Survivir

Surviving Life

Contemplations of The Soul

by
Brian Hunter

Wizard Way
Published by
Rainbow Wisdom
Ireland

ISBN: 9798415108589

DEDICATION

This book is dedicated to all of those who have suffered and experienced pain but have endured despite it. You are an inspiration. May we all survive the pain we suffer from and may we all thrive and prosper. Where there is hope, there is life, and there is always hope if we look for it.

CONTENTS

CONTENTS

PREFACE

This book is all about freedom of thought and freedom of feelings.
While the thoughts, ideas, and advice in this book are meant to help
you, they are not meant as a replacement for professional medical
and mental health care. If you are experiencing serious mental illness,
or feel like you might harm yourself or others, please seek
professional help from your doctor or other mental health
professionals.

National Suicide Prevention Lifeline

1-800-273-8255

CHAPTER ONE

Read This First

If you picked up this book and opened it, it means you were meant to have it. It was crying out to you, and your soul was crying out for it. This book is not a trap, nor is it an obligation. Just hold it if and when you want to. Read it if and when you want to. Don't read it if and when you don't want to. But know that you were meant to have it.

You want to feel better. You want to be okay. You want to have a friend. You don't want to be lonely. You want to be inspired. You want a better life. You want hope. Maybe you want guidance. Maybe you just want to be amused.

This book is your new friend. I am your new friend. Sorry about that in advance. Here is the good news, though. If you get tired of me, you can simply put me down, and I will go quiet. Or maybe not. Some say they can still hear me in their head, after I have spoken through words and feelings. Sorry again.

I'm not that horrible, though. I'm well-meaning at least. I am a lot like you. I want to be okay. I want to feel good. I want things to be okay. I want to heal. I want a better life. We likely have a lot in common.

Like you, I have had my share of traumas and dramas. I have suffered many losses. I've suffered for years at a time. I have lived with little hope. I have seen people come and go, and I have been alone for various long periods of time. I get it. I understand. I cry inside all of the time, believe me.

So, what makes someone like me qualified to write a book like this? Does this mean I have to justify and prove my desire to write a book like this, or I am not allowed to do so? No. I can do it because I want to, and because I feel I have something to say that might help others. You could do the same as me. It just so happens that I'm the one sitting here listening to music while I type these words to you. So, let's just chat.

First of all, there are no rules. You do not need to read this book cover to cover. You do not need to read *all* of this book. You don't need to read any of it. You can do whatever you want. You are in charge. I wrote this book so that you can dip in and out of it randomly, and at will. Skip around. Find topics that interest you and open up to that page.

This book is a lot like going for a walk through the woods. Some things you might want to check out in depth, and other things you might want to just walk on by. It's okay. Pick through it. Get lost. Then try again another time. Revisit things you like as often as you wish and as often as you need to. Totally ignore other things that don't serve you.

I just want you to feel that you are not alone. I want you to know you have a friend. You need to realize that someone wants you to feel better. I do. I want you to feel better.

Why? Am I just full of crap for saying that? I might not even know you. Why would I care if I don't know you? Am I just saying more bullshit that people say when they are trying to be nice? People are always talking bullshit. I get tired of it. Don't you?

Look. The answer is simple. I care about you feeling better,

10

because for me that is part of living a meaningful life. A decent person wants others they do not even know to feel better. That statement is so simple that it sounds stupid. But yet, how many people do you know in this world care about how strangers feel?

Okay, I will give you another reason why I want you to feel better. My first reason was too slick and general. My additional reason is that I have felt so much pain in my own life, that I literally want to eliminate it from the universe, almost out of revenge. I can't do that, but I can try. I don't want anyone to experience pain. I want everyone to experience peace and happiness. You having a better life does not take anything away from me. It costs me nothing. In fact, you being happy only enriches me all the more.

Giving to others, being generous, being kind, having compassion, and helping others, only makes each of us better. Why our society has made it seem like people have to earn these things first, and that giving to them takes away from what others have, I have no idea. It is society being mentally ill and lost, I suppose.

Anyway, sorry for rambling. I am going to ramble sometimes. Sorry in advance. This book is one long ramble. It's exactly like LIFE in that way. So let me get back on track.

This book is hoping to help you feel better. It is hoping to make your life better. That is the goal. *Surviving Life* is about feeling better. Thus, that will be the focus. But from time to time, I will attempt to give some practical advice that might help. I have helped many clients over the years with endless amounts of issues, and I have had my own share of traumas as well. I might have some useful advice. Keep what serves you and leave the rest behind.

With that said, I will say up front that I do not have all of the answers. Nobody does. I am just willing to admit it up front. Also, do as I say, and not as I do. I say this while laughing. Nobody is perfect, and certainly I am not. But I suspect that you might be able to utilize my advice and thoughts better than I can. So just keep an open mind to trying.

If nothing else, we will at least try to have some fun together as we banter around different topics and thoughts. There are no absolute correct answers. I will often just say things, and perhaps that will cause you to realize your own correct answers, which might be far better than mine. That is the idea. I am not trying to be right, or smarter. I am only trying to be helpful.

This shouldn't matter, but lately it seems to matter, so I want to address it up front. I feel being transparent is important. I strive to leave politics and religion out of discussions that involve helping all people become better, and helping people become free of pain and suffering. Some of you might interpret some of my statements or philosophies in a certain way. I will say up front that I am an 'Independent,' politically. So don't try to guess what I am, or which side I live on. I will be all over the place. I tend to disagree with most everything I see politically. I have my own notions of how we should do things and treat each other. Additionally, this book is neutral on religion. Your religion is your business, not mine, and I won't be making any definitive statements one way or another on religion. So basically, just relax. Let's chill and enjoy the conversations.

Let me also say that if you are here looking for a better life, or a better way of life, I might suggest that you check out my book series *Living A Meaningful Life*. Yes, this is an advertisement, and I am totally unashamed about it. Writing that book series changed my life, and maybe it can change yours also. I have written a lot of books, and I won't be mentioning many of them, but I am going to be mentioning that book series because it is so critically relevant to what we are trying to achieve in creating a better life for ourselves, with a better mindset. If you want to see some of my other books, you can find a list of them at the rear of this book.

Starting now, feel free to start thumbing through this book at whatever topics or chapter titles strike your fancy. Or just keep reading in order. That is fine also. I am happy you picked up this book, and that we get to spend this time together.

CHAPTER TWO

When You Think Nobody Loves You

Everyone wants to be loved. It is a human trait and need. But sometimes we just do not feel loved by anyone. Very often when we feel this way, it is due to a combination of attacks from multiple angles. Perhaps people close to us are being mean and hurtful. But at the same time, we might feel very alone and isolated from all others. It might even be that the world in general, full of all of its strangers, seem to be harsh toward us during those moments as well.

A skill of surviving life is to always be able to put things into proper perspective. When we are feeling hurt, or are in pain, we tend to get overly dramatic inside our own heads, and it just makes things worse than they have to be. So, when you feel like nobody in the world loves you, I would suggest you consider some of the following.

First of all, consider what triggered this feeling of yours. Did you get into a fight with someone? Are you feeling lonely in the moment? Usually when we get into a funk of feeling that nobody loves us, it is because we were triggered in some way. It is important that you stand back and recognize that you are feeling this way because of a specific triggering event, and that usually those events pass.

But sometimes they don't, and sometimes we truly feel unloved for a long period of time. If you are one of these people, then I need you to consider something. Please realize that the Universe/God always loves you. You are part of this creation we call Earth and humanity. Every person is meant to be here. If you were not meant to be here, you would not be here.

Think about when you take a walk within nature. Maybe there are trees, flowers, a stream, rocks, wildlife, or whatever the case may be. Each of those add to the beauty. Each flower, each leaf, each tree, they all add to the beauty. They all have a place there. They all have a purpose. They might not realize what their purpose is, and their purpose might be hidden amongst all of the other inhabitants of nature, but they each contribute to the beauty of it all.

This is how it is with people. Each person contributes to the beauty of humanity. Maybe you do not see it or realize it, but you do contribute to the beauty of the whole. This is ESPECIALLY TRUE if you are unique in some big way. Maybe you feel different, and you feel that you don't fit in. Maybe you think that because of how different you are, this is why certain people don't love you.

The way I see it, it is precisely your differences, and your uniqueness, that makes you contribute to the beauty of humanity that much more. When we are walking within nature, crowded with flowers, we do not notice any one flower in particular. We mostly appreciate all of the flowers as a whole. But each flower adds to the beauty of that entire scene, and we need each and every one of them there so that we can have the full picture of beauty. BUT, sometimes we see ONE weird looking flower. Perhaps it is very different than

15

the others in size, color, or shape.

We might think to ourselves, "Wow, *that* flower is WEIRD." That particular flower is sticking out amongst the crowd because it is so unusual. Some people might even say, "That flower doesn't belong there," or "How did that flower get there?" I suppose if the flower could understand the words of the humans, it might feel bad. To the flower, it would likely sound like the humans are saying it's weird and doesn't belong there. If I were that flower, and I heard those words, I would probably feel unloved in that moment. Anyone who says I am weird and don't belong somewhere probably doesn't love me, yes?

But is that really true? It is not. In fact, it is the opposite. That one strange flower is the one flower that captured the attention of the humans. Of all of the other flowers there, the unique flower is getting all of the attention.

Why is this? The answer is that things that are unique within a crowd, make things more interesting. And most people think that things that are interesting add to the beauty of a scene. This is not always true, and some people like everything the same. They tend to not be very artistic or open minded. That is just how they are. But so many others ARE open to learning new things and appreciating things that are different. Most of us have a little artist within us dying to get out.

Some regular flowers probably wish they were more unique so that they could get noticed more, and so that they could add to the beauty of the scene more. With that said, I remind you that ALL of the flowers are critically important to the beauty of the scene. But the weird unique flower is certainly incredibly important, as it is the one that catches our eye.

Once our walk is over, and we are back home, we may reflect upon our walk within nature that we took. What might we think of? Well, we will probably think about how beautiful everything was. We might think about how the walk made us feel. But one thing is for certain. We will definitely think of that one weird unique flower we saw while on our walk. It will be one of the highlights of the adventure. Thank goodness for that weird flower, because of all the beauty we saw during our walk, it was that weird flower that struck us the most, as far as how beautiful nature can be.

So, if you are *that* weird flower, God bless you. If you are one of the more ordinary flowers, God bless you. We need you all. You are all part of the beauty of nature, and specifically, humanity. You are beautiful, just the way you are, however you are.

But there's more. Humans have a design flaw. Humans seem to require validation for their value and beauty from outside sources. Humans do not just like to be loved because they enjoy the feeling of love. Humans like to be loved because that is their source of outside validation that tells them they are worthwhile.

Without being loved by an outside source, such as other people, humans often do not feel of any value to the world. This is why it can be so devasting to people when they feel that nobody loves them. Not feeling loved is bad enough, but worse yet is the feeling that you are not worthy or valued by humanity and the world. "If nobody loves me, then why am I bothering to be here?"

This is the question many people ask themselves, and it is the question that often leads to suicidal thoughts. This need to be validated, through love, by outside sources, is a design flaw. I might even call it a mental illness. But it is a mental illness that most humans share and suffer from.

Let us go back to the flowers for a moment. Imagine if no humans had walked through that part of nature which I described previously. Imagine if no humans had seen all of those flowers. Imagine if no human had seen that one weird unique flower. Would that make all of those flowers any less beautiful?

Does a human have to see something, and comment on it, in order for it to be beautiful? Do all of those beautiful flowers require a human to validate that they are indeed beautiful? Or can the flowers just exist, as they are, without any witnesses, and still be beautiful?

Fortunately for the flowers, and nature in general, they do not have the flaw that humans have. They do not require outside validation to prove their worth and value. Thank God for that. Imagine how painful and horrible it would be to be a flower and require outside validation of your value. Imagine if you required others to love how you look. Imagine if you required this feeling of needing to be loved, or you felt useless and pointless. How horrible would that be?

Well, it would be just like being a human, I guess. I am sure that flowers and all facets of nature, are grateful every day that they are not human. Why would they want the requirement of needing validation from others to prove their worth?

Perhaps it is time for us to become more like flowers. Maybe we should start recognizing our own importance within humanity, as one of the flowers that make the entire thing beautiful. Perhaps we should realize that whether we are one of the more ordinary flowers, or one of the weird unique flowers, we play an important role in the beauty of the entire scene.

More importantly, perhaps we should realize that we are beautiful and important whether or not anyone sees us on their nature walk. We do not need outside validation to be beautiful. Yes, it is still nice to be loved. It is nice to be adored. It is nice to be admired and appreciated. It always will be nice to have those things. But it should not be a requirement for our existence. We are beautiful and necessary even without those sources of outside validation.

Besides, always remember that you are loved by nature and

humanity as a whole, just as all of those flowers are loved by the entire collection of flowers around them. Each one is part of the whole. When some get damaged, "the whole" gets damaged. The flowers might not know each other, or even communicate, but they are still part of the 'one' beauty of nature.

This brings us to the next step in the evolution. Self-appreciation. Or self-love. If you realize, understand, and believe all that I have said up to his point, then you should understand that it is time to love yourself. Each flower recognizes its own importance, and so should you. You are beautiful and necessary, even if nobody is there to notice, and even if there is no outside validation confirming it.

Why can't you appreciate your own beauty and contribution to nature and humanity? Why can't you accept the fact that you are part of the whole, and that your existence helps to make everything more beautiful? Why can't you love yourself for these facts? You should.

Never mind what others say. Never mind what people who are angry say. Never mind if nobody notices you. Never mind if nobody verbalizes validation of your beauty and worth. It is not totally necessary. None of these things affect your value in the universe. You do not need outside validation. You do not need people to adore and love you in order to be necessary and beautiful.

You are beautiful because you are here. Love *that*. Love your own beauty. Love who you are. Love your ordinariness or uniqueness. You are an important part of the whole. You are needed. The universe and nature love you, and need your existence. I need your existence. I am a student of humanity. I study humanity constantly. I find most interesting, the beautiful souls who feel they are alone, who maybe feel unloved, but yet they endure. That kind of strength gives me inspiration. Watching you makes me feel like I can be okay if *you* are able to be okay. And even if you are not okay, you are still fighting. That inspires *me* to keep fighting. It inspires everyone, even if they don't say anything.

So really, you are loved anyways, even if you do not know it or see it. You might feel alone, but you are not alone. So many others suffer with you and feel the same as you. They might be flowers in a different part of the forest. But they are going through the same stuff that you are going through, although in slightly different ways of course.

The truth is that we are all unique in some way, some more than others. But we all have our lonely moments when we feel weird, unique, and alone. But we are not alone. We are part of the beauty of humanity of the whole. I hope you decide to be one of the more beautiful parts of humanity. Don't be the thing that causes a bite or a rash. Be the part of humanity that people find inspiring and can appreciate the uniqueness and beauty. They might not say anything to you. They might only reflect upon it silently to themselves. But people love to see things, and people, that inspire them.

So, in those moments of hurt and loneliness, when you think that nobody loves you; know that you are wrong. You are always loved.

CHAPTER THREE

What Is Your Purpose On This Planet?

I think one of the major questions most humans ask is, "Why am I here?" "What am I supposed to do here?" "What is my purpose?" People often ask these questions in frustration, because they are struggling or suffering on some level, and they are wondering what the point of it all is.

This is very similar to the question of, "What is the meaning of life?" I would say the meaning of life and your purpose on this planet are linked. So, we can examine both of the questions at the same time. I discuss at greater length the topic of "the meaning of life" in my book *EVOLVE*. In this book, I am going to approach the question more from the angle of what our purpose is here on Earth.

Is our purpose to work a job? Is that why we were born on Earth? We are here to work for businesses, even if it is our own business? Is our purpose to suffer trauma and pain from bad things that happen to us here on Earth? Those two things seem to be what many humans spend most of their time dealing with, so that is why I am sarcastically suggesting them.

Some people call me cynical because I am a realist, but I am not *that* cynical, really. I don't believe we are here to just work and suffer trauma. Work is a result of how humans structured their society. Trauma is also partly a result of how humans structured society. But trauma is also a biproduct of having strong human emotions.

Humans have very strong emotions, and they are very easily triggered, and often in a very negative way. Of course, emotions are also triggered in wonderful ways. I believe our emotions are part of our purpose.

What I mean by that is that emotions are meant to be experienced and are meant to intensify all of our experiences here on Earth as humans. Think of it this way. Imagine watching your favorite movies, except without having any emotions. Would your favorite movies mean anything to you if you felt no emotion watching them? No. Your movies would only be images on a screen consisting of action sequences. The dialogue would just be words for communication. The movie would be boring and meaningless because it would not affect you in any way. You would not FEEL anything while watching it. We watch movies because they entertain us, but they do this by causing us to FEEL things. Movies activate our emotions. The more a movie activates our emotions, the better the movie is considered to be. Amazing movies make us feel things on a very deep level. That is what makes the movie so good.

So, what is the purpose of a movie? Entertainment is the easy answer, but the real answer is that the purpose of a movie is to activate our emotions. If it does not do this, it is considered to have failed in its purpose.

What does this have to do with anything we are discussing? Why am I talking about movies? Well, it is an analogy and example of what OUR purpose is here on Earth. I believe one of our major purposes of existing is to experience our emotions. I believe emotions and sensations are the greatest and most unique gifts that humans possess. It certainly isn't intelligence or kindness. No offense. Humans are lacking in many areas, such as the two I just mentioned, but emotions and the ability to experience sensations are not traits humans are lacking.

I believe humans are 'kings of the universe' when it comes to emotions. So much so that humans usually cannot control their emotions. They have emotions in that much abundance. It is overwhelming.

You also saw me mention sensations. Sensations are a sibling to emotions. Emotions are felt mentally, and sensations are felt tactilely. Both are FELT. As far as sensations go, there are obviously the senses or sensations of taste and smell that are very powerful for humans. A human can taste something and literally have a full body sensational experience. That is powerful if you think about it.

But my favorite example of powerful human sensations is that of sex. The sensations experienced during sex can be off the charts. God, the Universe, or whoever you believe our creator is, obviously wanted to "gift" humans with the most intense and powerful sensations that our bodies could handle. Sexual sensations are the strongest. A man or a woman at their peak of a sexual experience appear to be in some kind of convulsive pain, because the experience is so overwhelming and powerful. I rest my case on that one.

Emotions are the most problematic issue that humans have to contend with. Emotions can cause us great positive euphoria, but they can also cause us incomprehensible pain. It is that last part that causes humans the most pain and suffering. Most humans cannot handle an overload of negative emotions. It is a design flaw, and I will be submitting a lengthy complaint when my time here on Earth is done. So don't worry, I got your back. Hopefully after "they" review my complaints, all of you who are still here will see some improvements and upgrades due to my complaints and suggestions.

Or maybe not.

Gosh, I feel like I keep getting off track. Whenever I do that, just give me a nudge and I will get the hint. What does all of this have to do with your purpose here on Earth?

Well, if your purpose on Earth is not to work and earn money, and it is not to suffer in pain from trauma, then what could it be? For me the answer is clear. One of your main purposes here on Earth is to have the full human experience. The full human experience is defined as the experience one has as a human. That is defined as partaking in the most unique and powerful features which a human possesses. Emotions and sensations.

I believe your purpose on Earth is to EXPERIENCE things. It is to DISCOVER things.

You can read that last sentence again. Experience and discovery are what it is all about. Your purpose is to experience and discover all things that humans are capable of experiencing and discovering. These things will usually directly relate to emotions and sensations.

Discover your feelings. Experience your feelings. Figure out what evokes the most powerful emotions within you. Find new emotions, and nuances to existing emotions. Discover new ways that your emotions and sensations can be activated. Discover new ways in which your emotions and sensations can be activated to higher and more intense levels. Figure out how to engage all human emotions and sensations such that your mind and body react to them in incredible ways, in perfect synchronicity.

I really think that is the bottom line. Everything else you might think of as far as your "purpose" goes, can be linked back to the idea of you seeking to discover and experience emotions and sensations. Let's go through some examples.

Some people think their purpose is to find love. Their purpose is to find the perfect romantic partner, fall in love, and stay in love.

Okay, fine. But this mission of falling in love is only a means to an end. The "end" being to experience certain strong emotions that result from being in love.

Others might think their purpose in life is to become rich and successful. Well, okay. That's fine. But again, the end result of your success, fame, and fortune, is that you are HOPING it will result in some sort of intense euphoric rush of emotional satisfaction. You are thinking that your success will give you an "emotional high." It may or may not. But the point is that you are seeking this goal in hopes of experiencing a certain set of emotions. So again, it comes down to emotions.

Some people might say, "My purpose is to make a difference in the world," or "I want to have children," or "I want to feel a sense a great accomplishment," and so on. All of those things result in emotional experiences. No matter what you come up with, and no matter what you try to throw at me in rebuttal, it will always come down to you seeking to experience some sort of emotion or sensation.

Therefore, I submit to you as my closing argument, that your purpose on this Earth is to discover and experience emotions and sensations, regardless of which "means" you use to reach that "end." I rest my case.

With all of that said, you can disagree. Plenty of you will. Believe me, I read plenty of people's comments of what they think of me and my opinions, and I am well aware of the hordes of people who disagree and have their own ideas. It's fine. I love that we all are different and have different opinions and ideas. I respect that. Take my opinions and apply them to yours or throw them in the garbage. But either way, I stand by what I feel, and what I believe.

The next logical question might be, "What am I supposed to do with this knowledge?" People might remind me that they are stuck here on Earth, their circumstances are less than ideal, some might say their circumstances suck, while others will say that they can't experience emotions or sensations because of their circumstances. Maybe some people are working all of the time, or always caring for others. Maybe others are in pain mentally or physically because of trauma or illness. These reasons might limit a person's ability to discover and experience the emotions and sensations humans seek.

Those are all good points. However, they do not change your purpose. Humanity can twist themselves into a pretzel to try and construct a society that suggests different types of purposes, but it does not change the fact that humanity consists of humans, and a human's purpose is based upon experiencing emotions and sensations.

Your challenge, should you choose to accept it, and you indeed have no choice, is to somehow reconcile a human's core purpose as I have outlined it, against the confines of the society and circumstances in which you find yourself.

That statement above could be called a "mission statement." Your mission is to fulfill your purpose within the confines of your many restrictions and limitations placed upon you by society and your personal circumstances. Can you handle that? It's okay if you say no. Sometimes I don't think I can handle it either. But really, we have no choice. Therefore, we might as well face up to it, and get on with it.

So, let's say your life is great. You are rich, have a great family, and have freedom to do whatever you want. Wonderful! I'm jealous, but in a good way. Your suggested mission would be to use your advantages to MAXIMIZE your adventure of discovering and experiencing emotions and sensations.

It is not as easy as it sounds, though. Privileged people often discover very quickly that many of the things that they thought would give them emotional satisfaction, don't. People can feel empty and

26

disappointed. Many have a thought of, "Is this all there is?" This can often lead to depression because the person feels that life offers them nothing more than what they already have.

People often wonder why folks with seemingly perfect lives still fall into depression, behavioral problems, and addiction problems. The answer is a combination of bad influences, overwhelming societal or work pressures, and the possibility that they have reached the pinnacle of life, and that it can't get better for them, thus it can only get worse. Depressing thought. That is why some struggle.

My advice for those folks is to stay focused on the idea of experiencing the most positive and intense emotions possible. In my humble opinion, feel free to disagree, but a great way to achieve new emotional highs, is to reach out and make a difference for others who struggle. Having the power to affect other people's lives in such a quick, powerful, and positive way, results in an emotional highway more powerful than any drug can offer.

In other words, the emotions you are seeking are likely found by affecting the lives of others, instead of your own. I still recommend tasting the best foods, traveling the world, and trying new activities. But after that is said and done, you will find there are powerful and satisfying emotional experiences to be had in seeing the sudden smile and surprise on the face of a child or adult who is offered a new opportunity, or something they need, which they thought they could not get. You will discover a new set of emotions and sensations in doing this that you did not think existed.

I want to make it clear that I am not telling or suggesting what others should do with their resources, time, or energy. People can do what they want. It is their prerogative to give or not give. I am just making suggestions from my own experiences and knowledge. But my final point on this facet of our discussion is that it does not matter how amazing and perfect your current life is, your purpose is still the same as everyone else's. It is to discover and experience emotions and sensations.

Now, for those in the cheap seats up in the back, whose lives are not so perfect, or maybe even suck, let's all chat about us now. Let's say you struggle. Perhaps you suffer from pain and trauma. Maybe your circumstances keep you confined, restricted, and limited. Have I covered enough horribleness?

For all of us who are more in *that* camp, your mission is still the same. It is to discover and experience emotions and sensations. The great thing about the universe is that despite any artificial, societal, and economic restrictions placed upon you, nobody can take away your humanity. What I mean by this is that you still get to keep your ability to experience emotions and sensations.

In fact, I bring good news to you. Those who experience more pain and struggle, usually experience more intense and euphoric emotions when things go well. This is because your mind is used to enduring negative emotions, so when the positive emotions come around, your experience is usually going to be much more intense due to the contrast. That is an advantage of being disadvantaged.

Your purpose is to find and accept opportunities to experience as many emotions and sensations as possible. But you want to be sure you keep a good balance between positive and negative. You likely already have had your fill of negative experiences. So, focus on ways to have positive experiences. You might be thinking, "Duh," but it's not as obvious as you think. The reason is that most people who are mired in negative circumstances and emotions, tend to "shut down" and forego experiences all together, even if they are positive. So, it's not obvious. You need to make a conscious choice to reach out, go out, and take actions to accept new experiences.

The magic is usually hidden in the small things. Those small things are usually hidden within other people, or within nature. Therefore, regardless of your circumstances, look within those around you for hidden opportunities to experience precious moments. It does not matter if it is your romantic partner, child, coworker, or a random stranger. Always look within them for concealed opportunities at having some kind of meaningful interaction. Inside these interactions are very often gems of emotional surprises and rewards.

People with children know what I am saying. But you would be surprised at how many of these gems are hidden within interactions with strangers as well. Many people are going through some of the same things that you are. They might be struggling, and maybe they are even having a hard time precisely in the moment in which you encounter them. A random and kind interaction can often result in emotional relief, as well as a feeling of brotherhood or sisterhood as well. A pleasant smile, nice word, or positive gesture of some sort can lead to a satisfying human interaction which you might not have expected. Sometimes people even become friends this way.

If people are not your thing, then you can find the same living surprises of emotional inspiration within nature. But you have to go outside to find them. Yes, I just said that. Yes, some people need to be reminded that nature is found OUTSIDE. So go outside. Discover nature. Discovering nature will usually evoke positive emotional responses at some point.

Here is my advice and the point I am trying to make. If you are stuck in negative emotions and circumstances, you MUST reach out, and seek out, positive experiences. This is not a suggestion. This is a requirement for your health and survival. This book is called *Surviving Life*. If you want to survive life, you will need to learn to actively reach out and pursue positive emotional experiences, or you will suffer, and might not make it. So please heed my advice. Lots of things I say in this book are little bits of inspiration and ideas, but a few things are necessary skills, and this is one of them.

So, if you are sitting at home thinking about how your life is without purpose, or you don't know what your purpose is, this chapter is attempting to get you to realize that your purpose is to LIVE LIFE and have all of the experiences you possibly can, as they relate to emotions and sensations. All of this is despite any difficult circumstances you are living under.

It's as simple as that. When you are on your death bed, you won't be thinking about how you wish you had a different job, or a big house. Instead, you will be thinking about how you fully experienced life or didn't experience life. Once we are on our death bed, we all become equal. Rich or poor, privileged or disadvantaged, the playing field levels out. All people at that point ask themselves the same question. Did they live life? Each person will have to answer that question for themselves, and regardless of the person's advantages or disadvantages, each person will have a different answer.

Be the person that answers in the affirmative, that you had many meaningful experiences. Know that you experienced the full range of human emotions and human sensations. If you didn't, then did you waste your time as a human? Maybe. Might "they" send you back here to try again? You can answer that for yourself, depending upon your own beliefs regarding such things.

Some of you might want to come back again and repeat the perfect life which you have been currently living. But others of us would prefer to reshuffle the deck and try for better luck next time around in a different life. Most of us do not want to repeat the same things over and over. We want to discover new experiences. Wait, isn't that our purpose for being here? Why, yes, it is!

If after reading this chapter you still feel lost and confused about your purpose in life, it means that you did not get what I said. It most likely means that your brain is programmed to think that it needs to be doing something. Your brain thinks that your purpose is to be "doing something." Let me remind you that the purpose is to EXPERIENCE and FEEL things. That does not always mean "doing things."

So, in your confusion, think carefully about why you feel your purpose means you need to be *DOING* something. Maybe this is where you are going wrong. This might be why you feel lost. You are searching for something to *DO*, and that is not the answer to the question.

The answer lies within what you experience and feel. That comes first. Then next, you might "do something" in order to experience and feel something. But you have to get those priorities in the correct order, or you will remain confused. This is why people are so confused about their purpose. They are always thinking in terms of 'what to do,' rather than what they want to feel.

Ask yourself, "What do I want to feel?" That answer will then lead you to what you should be *doing*. Once you have the order correct, you should feel less lost.

The purpose is to experience and feel human emotions and sensations. Doing this successfully will result in you having feelings of accomplishment, fulfillment, and will put you more at peace. Only after you digest that, should you consider what things to do, that will result in you experiencing your desired feelings.

Okay, this was a good talk. I hope I clarified things better toward the end here. If you need to, reread the entire chapter, but honestly, you probably just need to revisit the last part of this chapter whenever you feel lost like you should be "doing something."

Live out your purpose by seeking out experiences, emotions, and sensations. DO the things that will result in the experiences, emotions, and sensations that you seek.

Your purpose is important. It is a great privilege, and a curse, to be human, and it is up to you to make the most of it. Your soul will be talking about your experiences here on Earth for many millenniums to come. Make sure your soul has some good stories to tell.

31

How Can You Feel Good?

Many of us ask ourselves, "How can I feel good again?" Some people are not even that lucky, and they ask, "How can I feel good?" Meaning, maybe you think you have never felt good, ever. Maybe you do not even know what "good" feels like.

What *does* "good" feel like? Feeling good is when you are laughing with friends whom you love and trust, while not having a care in the world. Feeling good is when you are lost in your favorite music, while the world does not intrude on your moment of peace. Feeling good is when you are in nature and you feel like you belong, just as you are, who you are.

Feeling good is a state of being. But feeling good depends on two factors. It depends on what you gravitate toward, and what you are able to block out. Go toward the light and block out the darkness.

What can you go toward? Go toward the light. What lights up your heart? Certain friends? Nature? A hobby? Animals? Music?

Certain activities? There are things that give light to your soul. Think about what they are. What makes you laugh? What gives you hope? All of these things are of the light. When you touch them, you are touching light that will warm your soul.

What must you block out to feel good? Toxicity. Block it out. Toxicity consists of people who make you feel bad. They are constantly pouring poison onto your soul. You will never feel good with those people around.

Who are these people? Well, they COULD BE family, friends, romantic partners, co-workers, and strangers who you come across in public. Why are they so toxic? Why are they so mean?

Most often, these people don't fully realize they are toxic. They are likely toxic because other people have filled them with toxicity, and now they are dumping their sewage all over you to get rid of it. Or, they are miserable, and they know it. In that case, they are toxic because making others as miserable as they are, makes them feel better.

But toxicity can also come from within ourselves. If you have suffered from trauma and other emotional issues, you possibly have plenty of toxicity within yourself that manifests in the form of negative self-talk that tears yourself down and makes you feel smaller than you are. Some people are their own worst enemy. If you are toxic to yourself, that needs to be addressed.

But let's keep it positive for a moment. Let us focus on how we can feel good by going toward the light of what makes us feel good. This leads us to the first question of, "WHAT makes us feel good?" We cannot figure out how to feel good unless we know WHAT makes us feel good.

When I work with clients on this issue, the first question I ask them is, "How do you want to feel?" The correct answer is not, "Good." The correct answer can be a variety of things, but it would be things like, "I want to feel loved." "I want to feel secure." "I want to feel accomplished." "I want to feel at peace." "I want to feel inspired." "I want to feel euphoric."

Those are all valid answers, and it is up to each person how they want to feel. You would be surprised at how many people cannot answer the question. They have no idea how they want to feel. The fact that they cannot pinpoint an answer to the question explains why they don't feel good. It is hard to feel good when you do not know *what* makes you feel good.

I cannot tell you what makes you feel good. You need to give this some thought and figure this out on your own. But I *can* give you some hints of inspiration. And *that* is my hint. "Inspiration." Many people feel good when they are inspired. Inspiration breeds hope. Hope makes us feel better. But I want you to feel GREAT.

What makes many people feel great is the feeling of love. Love for someone, love from someone, and love for oneself, makes us feel great. The first two are somewhat out of our control and can come and go. The sure-fire stable one to shoot for is love for oneself. If you are comfortable with yourself, then you have a good chance of feeling good, if not great.

How do you feel good about yourself? You do this by *BEING* what inspires you. So, what kind of person inspires you? Adventurous? Kind? Ambitious? Generous? Powerful? Active? Reflective? You get to choose. I am trying to remain neutral and not project my own values upon this choice. There is no *one* correct answer. The only requirement is that you choose the one that inspires you the most, and then fully commit to BEING *that*. Notice I did not say "aspire" to being that. I said BE that.

What do we have so far? To feel good, you need to block out toxicity, and then go toward the light of what inspires you. Decide how you want to feel, what you want to be, and then BE it, even if it is only on a tiny scale at first.

34

It would have been so much easier if I had said that you can feel good again by taking a walk within nature and thinking happy thoughts. While that is helpful, I simply believe that life is more complicated than that. I also think life is more difficult than that.

There is so much toxicity floating around, that the task of dealing with toxicity alone can be an overwhelming job. But you need to dredge it out and clear your soul of as much of it as possible. It's all dirty and does not belong within you. You have to take out the trash first, before you can expect your home to smell beautiful.

But then you have to look up toward the sun. See the light. Let it into your heart and soul. Then think about what inspires you. LIVE. Living life means doing what inspires you or engaging in your passion.

Being inspired by something, engaging in that as a passion, and BEING the person that inspires you, will all make you feel good. That is a close description of your final destination. Now think about where you are currently, in relation to that final destination. Perhaps you are close, perhaps you are well on your way, or perhaps you have a long way to go. But now you have a direction to go in.

Regardless of how long you think that journey might be in your specific case, you can feel better today by beginning your process of blocking out, and rooting out, the toxicity in your life, and in your heart, soul, and mind. Then you can also begin immediately BEING more like the person that inspires you. It's okay to start small, as long as you start.

You CAN feel good. But you have to go back to basics and do the work required. Do not give up on the idea of feeling good, and do not give up on yourself. I believe you can do it.

CHAPTER FIVE

Finding Joy

Everyone wants to find Joy. Where is she? Where is she hiding? The Joy I know lives in the United Kingdom. While she is a wonderful lady, we are here to talk about a different joy.

We are looking for the joy that we know of as happiness. We want to live with joy in our hearts. We want our lives full of joy. We want to be happy.

How can you find joy?

Are you asking me?

As if I know?

Here is the problem with looking for joy, and actually finding joy. Joy can be tricky and fleeting. You can capture joy for a period of time, but then it slips away as quickly as you found it. The big chase would be on.

Maybe look in all of the popular places where joy can be found? Perhaps find a person to be with who will love you? Enter into a relationship to find joy? Maybe another person can give you joy? Is that the secret trick?

Certainly, there must be a way to find someone to give you joy? Or a place we can go to find it?

Yeah, no. Let's stop playing. Looking for joy in all of the wrong places, and even in all of the right places, will still leave you disappointed in the long run. Why is that?

Joy should not be chased, only to be captured and held captive for a short period of time, for us to then lose it again.

What am I suggesting then? Am I suggesting that joy cannot be chased, found, and captured? Am I saying that we should just give up on joy? Am I that cynical? Maybe. But no. I am not.

Joy is not something that can be chased, captured, and held. Joy is not something that we should be depending on others to give us. There is only one true way to find and have joy in your life. It is to create the joy. Become the joy. Or at least bathe in it. Breathe it.

What even *is* joy, anyway? Joy is when your heart sings. It is when you are not feeling trauma. Yes, my definition of joy is when you are not feeling trauma. How wonderful is that? It is joyous, that is how wonderful it is.

So, while joy equals happiness, it is more complex than that. It is a state of relaxed being where all trauma has been set aside, and your heart is free to be, and to sing its favorite songs.

Do you want to feel joy? Meaning, do you want to not feel any trauma? Which came first, the chicken or the egg? By the way, I answer that exact question in detail in my book, *EVOLVE*, but I digress. The question at hand is whether joy comes from the lack of trauma or is it the lack of trauma that creates joy. The answer is: both. They are a mirror image. No trauma equals joy.

Yes, there are different levels of joy. There is euphoric joy, which is fleeting and rare, but there is also stoic joy which might not show on your face, or in your mood, but you feel the joy of peace within you. I like this kind of joy a lot. Feeling peace in my heart while in a state of relaxation without trauma, is the best kind of joy for me. One of the biggest reasons is that it doesn't have to be fleeting. It is not created by brain chemicals. It is created by current circumstances. In other words, it is real and sustainable.

Remember how we were just discussing the idea of chasing joy? I said it is not a good method. This is why. Joy is not about grabbing something and holding it. Joy is about creating and building a state of joy within yourself that can be lasting.

A big part of that is creating a space where you can set all trauma aside. Since joy is the lack of trauma, we need to set aside the trauma. No trauma equals joy.

How do we set aside trauma? The long answer is that we do a long period of self-work to resolve the trauma. But for the sake of this chapter, let's discuss the short answer instead. While you work on resolving your trauma, you should develop coping mechanisms that allow you to set aside your trauma, at least temporarily. Finding these coping mechanisms will be your key to joy, at least in the short term.

For example, engage in activities that allow your mind to disengage from trauma. Many people find relief by exercising, being in nature, spending time with good-natured friends, listening to music, and engaging in hobbies. Find hobbies that cause your mind to stop thinking in its normal patterns. What I mean by this is find hobbies where you stop thinking of trauma-triggering thoughts.

When people do certain chores, like house cleaning or grocery shopping, they very often do those tasks while thinking about their other problems and issues. The person gets triggered by thinking of these issues, and they are then living within their trauma. I am suggesting hobbies and tasks which do not allow your mind to do the multitasking of thinking of other problems and issues that will trigger you. Some examples might be reading, painting, playing games, or other such things that require your full concentration.

Okay, so we have this part down, right? Find things to engage in that allow you to set aside trauma. It's not that simple, though. Being unhappy, and then sitting down to work on a puzzle, is not going to give you joy. What is needed is for you to detach from your trauma for longer periods of time, over time. You need to recondition your mind to enjoy being without trauma for decent amounts of time.

This means restructuring your lifestyle. You need to change your lifestyle in such a way that it includes many coping mechanisms that drown out trauma. It also requires you to change how you respond to triggering events.

Some of you might be thinking, "I can't change my lifestyle enough because I have to work. I can't quit my job." Yes, true. I understand. This is why I am bringing up this notion of changing how you respond and react to triggering events. Along with your increased number of coping mechanisms in your daily life, you also need to change your response to triggering events, while you are having to be in environments that you can't eliminate, such as your job, or such as dealing with certain toxic people.

The best way to change your response to triggering events, is to not respond at all. There might be certain things that happen to you, or are said to you, that trigger you into a trauma response, and cause you to react poorly. The change you are seeking to make at this time is to stop responding to these triggering events. Let's say the triggering event, or words, happen. Stop. Breathe. Say to yourself, "No." Say, "Doesn't exist. Not valid. Toxic. I reject that." Then physically turn your head away in another direction. Emotionally block it. Your actual response to the person might be to say, "Okay." You will acknowledge them in a way that makes them think you have accepted and processed the triggering event. But emotionally you have blocked it and won't be processing it. It's invalid. Why would you process it?

You won't.

Don't.

This all takes practice. But try it. Keep trying it. At a certain point, the magic takes hold. The magic is that the triggering event no longer controls you. Triggering events no longer own you. They bounce off of you. It was a conscious decision of yours to no longer accept such triggering events as valid things to process. If you don't accept them, and you don't process them, then they no longer trigger you like before.

With triggers being disarmed, those triggers are no longer effective in activating your trauma. Without your trauma responses and deep trauma being activated, you can start to feel joy on an increasing level. Why? Well, because without trauma, joy can exist. Joy is having no trauma. No trauma equals joy.

It takes time. It takes practice. You might need to read this chapter again, or a few times. It is a process of realization and a pathway of thinking. You have to see the entire thing clearly, develop your coping mechanisms, then change how you respond to triggering events. They all have to work, and they all have to work together. But you can do it.

There is one last piece of this that we need to bring up again and incorporate within us more deeply. It is the idea of BEING joy, rather than chasing it. I have kind of already discussed it, but it needs to be made crystal clear.

Joy is not something you chase and capture. Joy is something you become. It's a lifestyle thing. You have a lifestyle of joy by virtue of your choices in how you handle trauma in your life. This means you choose what activities make up your lifestyle, which people you interact with, and how you react to triggering events and toxic situations. These are choices and skills. You must actively manage all of this in order to create a lifestyle of joy. Creating a lifestyle of joy will result in you experiencing joy in your life. You will become what you build. Whatever lifestyle you build is what you will become. So, if you build a lifestyle of joy, you will become joy.

Once you become joy, you are joy. It can't be taken away. You will not depend on other people for your joy. This means that nobody can take it away from you. How wonderful is that? We call that independence. We call that self-empowerment. Sound good? It is good. It makes you a more powerful person. Be that person. Be a powerful person. Be a person of joy, because you are filled with joy. You will do it by building a lifestyle of joy. One step at a time, and you can be okay. It will be okay. Things can be okay, including your life. Your life can be great and full of joy.

CHAPTER SIX

Journey Over Destination

I have some unsolicited advice to offer. I offer this advice after having experienced life from all different sides of the table. I grew up poor, managed to create a successful life from nothing, then watched is all get stripped away. I've been rich and I've been poor. I've done amazing things, and I've also done nothing. I have felt euphoria, and I have felt great suffering for years at a time. I've had amazing people in my life, and I have lived life completely alone for periods of time.

I have learned some things from that dumpster fire burning onboard a trainwreck of a life I have had. I have learned that nothing is forever, everything changes, people change, people come and go, successes will be had, and failures will be had as well. Nothing will work out as you think, and some things you thought were nothing will turn into the most magical treasures.

There is plenty to talk about here, but I want to focus on the "debate" between the importance of "the journey" vs. the importance of reaching your desired "destination" in life.

When I was an older teen and young adult, I was fully focused on the DESTINATION. It is all I thought of. My thinking was that I was willing to endure any difficult journey in order to reach my final desired destination. I viewed the JOURNEY as a price to pay in return for reaching the DESTINATION. I did not put any value in the journey. All that mattered was that I eventually reached my desired destination.

Due to this thinking, my early journey was not very rich with experiences. It was rich with sacrifices and struggle. I didn't like my journey very much. But I was willing to endure my journey in the hope of finally reaching my destination.

In my particular case, my hard work paid off, and I eventually reached my desired destination. It felt good, and it felt fulfilling. Well, it felt this way for a short while, anyway. But the "reward" of reaching my destination was followed by a series of realizations and unexpected events.

First of all, I had a mental crisis at a very early age, having become successful at a very young age. My thought was, "Is this it?" "Is this all there is?" "Do I just keep doing this for sixty more years, and then I die?" It was a horrifying thought. I found myself bored of my success almost immediately after achieving it. My destination was wonderful, but I was "over it" very quickly.

It was similar to how some people buy a very expensive exotic car, and are very excited about it at first, but then eventually, it just sits in the garage unused. Or it is like the diamond jewelry we are so excited to receive, but then eventually never wear. Little kids go through the same thing when they receive a new toy which they really wanted, but before too long, they are "done" with it, and don't play with it much anymore.

Each of those examples above illustrate "destinations" that have been reached. When we finally receive something that we have wanted so badly, we are indeed excited and happy with ourselves for having finally reached it or received it. Each of those items are a "destination." It doesn't matter whether it's a "thing" you want, or a position in life, they are "destinations." You embark on a journey to achieve or attain that destination.

Much of the journey can be difficult, and all of it is made in an effort to reach a certain destination. But then, as I have outlined previously, the destination we reach might only provide a short-lived sense of true joy and satisfaction.

In my case, the destination was not just a car or jewelry, but it was "success." It was a pretty grand, significant, and important destination. But I became bored. My mind and spirit were way bigger than my destination, as it turned out. That was not the only surprise I would experience.

At some point, I had some very unexpected, unique, and unfortunate events hit me. These events, in close succession, also commonly referred to as "life," caused me to start to lose my "destination" that I had worked so hard to achieve. There was nothing I could do. It was life doing what life does. Eventually it was all gone.

I reflected upon the fact that I had sacrificed many things in life, and had endured an unpleasant journey, just so I could reach a destination that was quite quickly taken away from me. What a waste. What I mean by that is it was a terrible waste of a journey, in order to achieve a destination that was not lasting or worthwhile. I found myself wishing that I had enjoyed my journey more, even if it had been at the expense of the destination, since the supposed destination turned out to not be that great or sustainable anyway.

That was my first life confirmation that it is never worth sacrificing your journey for a destination. Life would continue teaching me such things. One of my many lessons would involve the realization of how difficult journeys can be more rewarding than wonderful destinations.

There was a time in my life, after I had lost everything, that I started to finally live life. I socialized more, engaged in more activities, and tried things in life that I had never tried before. Some of it was good, and some not so good. But all of it was a grand adventure. I struggled in life during that entire period, so the journey was rough. But as I look back on it, I also lived more during that journey, than I had previously lived in my entire life. My regret was not fully living my journey sooner.

I might also add that during this time of great adventure, I had NO destination in mind. I had totally given up on any destinations after my previous failures. Thus, that time of my life was 100% about the journey only. Although it was a very difficult time, I look back on that adventurous journey as "LIVING LIFE," as opposed to before when I was making my journey miserable and disposable, just so I could reach a destination.

Fortunately, as I became older, wiser, more tired, and more introspective, I developed an appreciation for balance in such matters. It is healthy to have positive destinations (goals) in mind, but never try to achieve them at the expense of your journey. Maybe read that last line again.

Perhaps that line is my advice to you. But there is more to it than that. I truly believe that life is more about "the thrill of the chase," than it is capturing your prey. I want to examine this notion.

When we chase after our dreams, the chase is the journey. The chase allows us the blessing of having HOPE that we might someday achieve it. It allows us the blessing of being excited each day to chase after what we truly want. We get to feel INSPIRED by our efforts toward what we want to achieve. We get to feel good about ourselves when we reach certain milestones on our way to reaching our destination. We feel a sense of satisfaction from having put in solid work toward a certain goal, and the satisfaction from getting

45

closer toward our goal.

Think about all of what I just said. I just explained in one paragraph what LIVING LIFE is supposed to be about. I didn't even mention the part about how we often get to be on this journey with others, who we build a bond with because of the journey. We also get to learn things along the way. There is no limit to the number of life-enriching moments and experiences that we can have specifically from the journey.

It is during this journey, that life happens. This is when all of your memories will be made. This is when relationships will foster and grow. This is when you will learn and grow as a person. This is when all of the magic of life happens.

So far, everything I have said is only in relation to the journey. The chase. Chasing the dream. Life. Living life.

Now let us look at the destination. Let's say that you finally reach the destination. Okay, great. Congratulations. Super. Good for you.

What now? I guess you enjoy your victory for a bit?

Hours, days, weeks, months?

Then what? What's next?

Hmmmm....

I guess that's all I have to say about reaching the destination. What else is there to say, other than good for you and congratulations?

I think it is wonderful to reach a destination, but it's pretty thin in terms of lasting gratification. I am starting to think that the journey is far richer in its value to a person's life.

I notice within many people the idea of them being totally focused on a destination. This is what is taught and preached in all of the motivational success books. The books are trying to help you reach a destination. They are trying to do their job.

I am not saying anything bad about those books. I am just saying that I do not think that people should be fully focused on just a destination. It is not healthy, and many people will find that they have wasted part of their life on this total focus on the destination, as the expense of their journey. I know, because I lived it myself.

I have learned that living a meaningful life means living a journey that is full of meaning, satisfaction, and inspiration, on a daily basis. Notice I did not say enjoyment. I will never promise you a rose garden, and I don't think life is easy and enjoyable all of the time, or much of the time. But that's the point. Despite my cynical statement about life being a struggle, I think it is important to live your daily journey in a way that you still feel some sort of inspiration, hope, meaning, and satisfaction. What I am saying is that you need to focus on your daily journey.

Focus.

On.

Your.

Journey.

Ideally, I would say to have a destination in mind, let it excite you, let it inspire you, let it make you smile at the thought of achieving it. But that is where your focus on the destination ends. After that, it should be all about the journey. Structure your journey carefully. Be constructive and healthy. But be sure to live your daily journey in a way that provides you with a reason to live each day.

Find joy in the small things. Find inspiration in hidden places. Get excited about things, however small they may be. Engage in actions that provide you with satisfaction, joy, love, and inspiration.

BE all of those things. Build your journey with those things. Make sure you try to feel all of those things every day. It's important. Your mental health is at stake. The health of your spirit is at stake. Self-care is everything. Without self-care, it is difficult to survive life.

While your destination is just a point off in the distance, your journey is your life. Your journey is what will determine if you feel you have lived life or not. Destinations are too fleeting to provide this. Plus, I have more bad news for you. Destinations most often change or never happen. Life has a funny and cruel way of changing our destinations. Life laughs at you. You should laugh back, knowing that you are no longer relying on your destination for your life validation.

The bottom line is that surviving life is all about finding ways to remain inspired and hopeful. But truly living, and living a meaningful life, is all about what we do on the journey. I would say that life is 90% journey, and 10% destination. That is just my own opinion. I know there are plenty of people, especially those readers of motivational books, who will totally disagree with me. I don't mind people disagreeing with me. Each person learns about life in their own way. All I can do is offer my own experiences and opinions. People can choose what to keep, and what to leave behind.

With all of that said, I truly believe that you will be a happier person, live a happier life, and live a more meaningful life, if you put more focus on your journey. Create a daily journey that is inspiring, meaningful, and enriching to your soul. If you don't have that now, then you have some work to do. You should do the work. It is totally worth it.

CHAPTER SEVEN

Living A Meaningful Life

W hat does "living a meaningful life" mean? Why, it is the title of my epic book series, of course. Duh. Okay, just joking. Not really joking. But we are not talking about my book series in this specific case. I want to talk about what that phrase really means, and what it means to you in your life.

It is safe to say that this chapter is related to the chapter called "What Is Your Purpose On This Planet?" This chapter could easily be a subset of that chapter. This is because we are seeking to live a meaningful life while we are attempting to live with purpose or live out our life purpose.

Everyone is entitled to create their own definition of what "living a meaningful life" means to them. But since I am the one tasked with writing this book, I am going to give you, *my* definition. You can decide for yourself if it works for you, or if you want to adapt my thoughts into your own thoughts to create your own definition. Whatever works for you is fine with me. I am feeling easy to get along with tonight as I write this. You are lucky you didn't catch on a bad night when I am feeling less cooperative. By the way my editors hate these personal comments in my books, but I don't care. It's just me talking with YOU. I feel we are friends by now, so it's fine.

Anyway, my own definition of "living a meaningful life" is living your life in such a way that you feel the most empathic satisfaction from how you are living. I have likely succeeded in making you more confused than you were before I gave the definition. I might need to clarify and expand my thoughts.

When we do meaningful things, it means that how we lived affected others, or the world, in a meaningful way. This means that we gave others something very positive through how we lived our lives. We may have given others what they needed, or we may have inspired others to do great things, which they may not have otherwise done. We may have given relief from suffering, or opportunity for pleasure, where there was little or none before we came along.

A better definition is to say that we lived our lives in such a way that contributed to the life purpose of ourselves and other people. This means that how we lived our lives allowed ourselves and others to have experiences which resulted in positive outcomes or emotions.

Who knew such a simple phrase would be so difficult to define? This might explain why I had to write an entire book series in an attempt to show what it means, through example.

To me, living a meaningful life is the opposite of living an empty life. Living an empty life is living a life where nothing matters. So, living a meaningful life would be living a life in which everything you do matters. Make sense?

The magic in successfully living a meaningful life is the ability to provide positive meaning and outcomes through even the smallest actions and gestures. For example, living a meaningful life would be showing kindness to someone, which in turn changes that person's day, or even their life. That kindness you showed was small and cost nothing, yet it had a powerful positive result. That's a great example of living a meaningful life.

Another example would be allowing yourself small pleasures in life that make you happy. They might be small things that seem insignificant, but they provide you with great comfort and happiness. Filling in your day with little things that give you comfort and happiness, is an example of living a meaningful life.

So, living a meaningful life means living in a such a way that you are constantly providing positive outcomes and inspiration to yourself and others. Another way to look at it is living your life in such a way that you are constantly engaging in self-care for yourself, but also caring for others as a way of providing comfort to them. Small sacrifices and gestures that result in much larger positive outcomes are definitely examples of living a meaningful life.

In my book series by that name, I mention how living in such a way means that you are living with integrity, decency, honor, generosity, compassion, and kindness. I believe this is true, and I believe this is the best way to accomplish living a meaningful life. However, for our purposes here, I don't want to cast judgment on how people live their lives, or how they choose to live a meaningful life. I only mention those traits as a way of leaving some bread crumb hints as a way of you heading down the right path.

The important point I don't want to get lost, is that living a meaningful life is often done in very small and subtle ways. You do not need to accomplish huge feats of miracles. For the most part, you only need to show kindness toward yourself and others. It is mostly about kindness. If you are kind to yourself and others, then it is very likely that you are on your way to living a meaningful life.

By living your life in a meaningful way, you are better assured of feeling a deep sense of satisfaction from your life. If you feel some satisfaction from your life, you are more likely to feel happy and content. We want you to feel happy and content. If you are feeling good about yourself and your life, it means you are doing a great job at surviving life.

CHAPTER EIGHT

When The World Is Crumbling Around You

I think most people can attest to this feeling sometimes, of the world crumbling around us. Whether it is literally the world, or more directly your immediate family, friends, or environment, it can feel overwhelming and steal your enthusiasm and hope when things seem to be in meltdown mode. Just watching the news is enough to send some people into a deep depression. It is hard to feel hopeful about your own future when you see on TV that the future of the world looks bleak.

How is a person supposed to survive their own harsh reality when everything around them is so depressing? I have a certain philosophy about all of this that I believe is the best and most effective way to navigate "global depression."

You should not spend too much time focusing on things which

you cannot control. If you don't control it, you can't fix it. It only makes logical sense to spend your resources on things which you have at least *some* control over and can perhaps be fixed. Worrying about things you cannot control is never a fruitful endeavor.

So, when the world around you has got you down, my suggestion is to INCREASE your focus on your own actions and behavior. By elevating your own values and behavior, you *CAN* change the world. The world is changed one person at a time. But EACH PERSON has to do their part.

Think about it. If each person always did the "right things," the entire world would be crawling with people who were all doing the right things. If this was happening, then the world would not be crumbling.

Almost all of the world's problems are a result of human behavior. You can possibly say that the only exception is natural disasters. However, even with natural disasters, life would be okay if each person did the right things in dealing with those natural disasters.

I am not going to place my judgement on what "the right things" are. I think it's obvious, but I am not going to argue with people who like to argue about the obvious. With that said, there are valid differences in opinion of some values, the prioritization of such values, and how such values are to be maintained and administered. Differing opinions are always fine. Humanity would be boring without differing opinions. I am just saying that I think most of us know deep down what "the right things" are, and we will leave it at that. Do "the right things" your own way, within your own belief system and culture. You get to decide what that is, not me or anyone else.

My point is that the most logical and effective action you can take against the hopeless sense of the world crumbling around you, is to respond by YOU taking your own action to BE and CREATE the world you want. You can empower yourself to take action and make a difference. Doing this will make you feel better about what is going on around you. You cannot control what others do, but you *can* control what *you* do.

I feel passionate about this approach, and it is the philosophy that my *Living A Meaningful Life* book series is based upon. This approach to life that I am suggesting is not just something 'cute' that I am saying for this chapter. I am fully invested in this life philosophy, as much of my work as an author has been based around it.

I think it is much harder to change things these days. It is hard to get others to change, perhaps impossible. But you have total control over *you* BEING THE CHANGE. If you live what you want to see in the world, then others will see this from you, and maybe they will decide that they want to live that way also. If enough people start to decide they want to live this way, then before long, you have more and more people living in a way that creates a better world. It all starts when one person, then others, start BEING THE CHANGE. It starts when you live in a way which you would like to see be the way of the world.

We will all never agree on how to live. That's fine. Don't force your ways on others, just like you don't want them forcing their ways on you. But you can choose to live in a positive inspiring way that inspires others to do the same IN THEIR OWN WAY.

Allow everyone the freedom to express this way of life in their own way. The important thing is that you live in a positive way that supports a more loving and productive society in which we can all prosper. You can figure out what that means to you, and what you would like to see for the world in your own visions and beliefs.

When the world has got you down, stop fixating on everything you cannot control. Look at yourself. What can YOU do to make a better world? BE THE CHANGE. Up your game. Treat people better if you think the world does not treat people well. Increase your own level of integrity if you think the world is lacking in integrity. Increase your own courage and strength if you think those qualities are what the world is lacking. Increase your own independent spirit, or your own level of innovation if you feel the world is lacking in them. Change how you interact and lead others, if you don't like how the world is being led.

BE THE CHANGE.

This is very empowering. You will feel like you are making a real difference in the world, and you will be making a huge difference by behaving this way.

Don't let everything crumbling around you drag you into the abyss. Instead, let it motivate you and empower you to be better. Be better! You can do it!

CHAPTER NINE

When They Are Disappointed In You

Have others said that they are disappointed in you? Or, even more likely, have they said nothing, but they give off the energy of being disappointed in you? Do family, parents, partners, or just society in general, give off vibes of being disappointed in you?

Why? Are you struggling? Have you experienced some setbacks? Have you experienced some things that did not work out? Perhaps you struggled to do what you thought was right, or maybe there were no "right" choices to begin with. Maybe you accepted the only choices available to you at the time.

Things didn't work out, or you are not happy with how things worked out, or your present circumstances. Isn't that bad enough? Nope. Not usually. Usually, we have to suffer with the consequences of our outcomes, AND we must suffer with the judgements of others in addition to that. We have to live with others looking at us with disappointment, or with the knowledge that they are thinking, "You are disappointing," while they look at us. Which is more painful, the disappointing outcome, or having to deal with others thinking of us in that way?

Most of us know that we should not allow others to label us or invalidate us in a negative way. That's what all of the self-help books tell us. But this does not stop us from feeling the pain inside of what others think of us.

We can't control what others do and think. Read that line again. People are going to think what they want about you. It doesn't matter how amazing and successful you are, or how messed up you are feeling about yourself right now. Other people will think what they want about you. There is nothing you can do about it. The sooner you surrender to this idea, the better off you will be. The sooner you will heal from past traumas in this area.

Your problems in life, your mistakes, your setbacks, your struggles; they are what they are. Some of them might be your fault, some might be only partly your fault, and some might not be any of your fault at all. These are all separate issues. What we are talking about now is how others think of you regarding these issues. We are discussing how others might seem disappointed in you, or YOU *FEEL* that they think this way about you.

Your actions which resulted in bad results are from something called 'life.' People make choices based upon their individual circumstances, and from the choices that were available to them at the time. Sometimes we choose well, and sometimes we do not. Life is a journey of these choices, and then the consequences that follow.

SEPARATE FROM THAT, are the random judgements and thoughts which others have toward you. THESE JUDGEMENTS ARE TOXIC. Read that line again, and then maybe again.

It is this toxicity that we must focus on for the purposes of this chapter. The FEELING that you have about others being disappointed in you IS TOXIC. It is making you sick. It is destroying your self-esteem. It is making you suffer in pain. It is making you mentally ill. It is preventing you from fully healing. This toxicity is preventing you from feeling okay.

This toxicity has to go. You cannot allow it to exist within you. Easier said than done? Maybe. But let's look at this "big bad-boy monster." I am not afraid of monsters, and neither should you be. Monsters are bullies. They feed off of our fears. They are about 10% fact, and 90% fear. Take away the fear, and you take away the food it needs to survive.

This toxicity monster is based upon the judgments, thoughts, and opinions of others. Remember, these monsters feed off of 90% fear. The judgements of others really don't matter. They are of no use to us. None. So, their power is based in fear. We fear what others think of us. We fear they might be right in what they think about us. Any way you slice it, it is all based in fear.

For that reason alone, all judgements and opinions against you should be dismissed. NOBODY has the full knowledge of your unique individual circumstances, such that they are qualified to judge you. Nobody. Think about it. There are people making judgements about you without having all of the evidence and facts. This would never work in court, and it should not work in life, or in your mind. Their accusations should be dismissed based upon the fact that they do not fully understand your situation and all of its surrounding circumstances.

With all of that said, let us once again refocus on the central issue. The initial assertion was that others look upon you with disappointment. You know deep down inside that the judgements are unfair. Why do you feel this way? You feel this way because THOSE PEOPLE judging you have NOT walked in your shoes. They do not understand your circumstances, struggles, and reasons for why you have done the things that you have done.

It's not fair. You feel that you have to accept these judgements of disappointment, even though you know there are extenuating circumstances for how and why these opinions may have come about.

This leads me to the next very important point. These judgements, opinions, and feelings of disappointment toward you are ACCUSATORY in nature. What I mean is that other's opinions of you are not based upon all of the facts and circumstances, as I previously mentioned. They are only ACCUSATIONS that others are making against you based upon the limited and skewed perceptions that they have of you and your circumstances.

People are looking at you, and your predicaments, and they are very quickly coming to a judgement against you based upon a very brief view of your visible circumstances. It's very inaccurate. But more importantly, it is very accusatory. It is accusatory because they are just accusing you of not living up to "their expectations and standards" based upon their completely invalid and unfair brief cursory view of your situation.

Add to this the fact that people who judge you in this way, will also naturally BLAME YOU for your current situation and circumstances. Why do they do this? They do this because that is what humans do. They blame. They were taught to blame by their parents, and others, so they pass on this behavior of having to blame people for things. It does not matter if the evidence is not there, or if their judgement is based upon a tiny amount of information. People will use the smallest shreds of evidence to come to their conclusion of who to blame, and for what to blame you.

Let us just take a moment to review. So far, we have people who came to a conclusion that they are disappointed in you. They came to this conclusion by using a lack of evidence, not knowing your full situation, and by having a need to blame. They very quickly accused you of being deserving of their disappointment. Plus, they do all of this even though their judgments of you do not matter in reality. They shouldn't matter.

The worst part of all of this, is that YOU believe them. You hear their disappointment. You feel their disappointment. Then you internalize it. You accept it as truth. Their disappointment and judgments toward you become a part of you. You seem to accept it as reality. You buy into it. You then own it.

But it's all garbage. ALL OF IT. It's simply garbage. They are accusing you of being to blame for your own situations and outcomes, regardless of all circumstances. They are making you feel like you DESERVE their disappointment. This is the height of toxicity, isn't it?

What garbage. I am so tired of other people having the power to judge you in such a way that it damages your self-esteem and damages your soul. Toxic!

Let's look at some truth. Here is some reality that people who love to blame others wouldn't like. I am going to give you an analogy.

You are a flowering plant. You are a plant, born of nature. You didn't ask to be born. You didn't ask to exist. But you do. Nature gave you life. Unfortunately, you need certain things to thrive. You need good soil, sunlight, water, and love. Without those things, you do not grow well, you do not survive well, and you most certainly won't flower.

Some of us are born into lovely circumstances. Some are born in a botanical garden, which has perfect growing conditions, and has constant attention from experts that make sure all of the plants are healthy and thriving. Life is good. The plants do great, and all of them flower. Duh. Why wouldn't they? When you have perfect conditions, it's easy to succeed and flower.

But others might be born into a very different and harsh environment. You might be born into a situation where the soil is horrible, there is very little water, and you are always shaded and don't get any sun. How will you grow? Not well. You will struggle. You do not have what you need to thrive. It's just a fact. You are born of nature, and you require certain conditions to thrive. If you do not have the benefit of being in those conditions, then you will struggle.

Did you ask to be put into a harsh environment? Do you like being in a harsh environment? Do you like being in crappy soil and never having water? No.

But watch this. As amazing as it seems, there will still be people who are disappointed in you for not thriving. They will accuse you of being LESS THAN others, because you are not thriving. They will accuse you and blame you for not thriving. They will wonder why you are not flowering. They will form an opinion of you that is not favorable.

Wait, it gets worse. Not only are you planted in a harsh environment where you can't thrive or flower, and you also get blamed for it, AND you WILL ALSO begin to believe their opinions of you. You will begin to feel like a loser for not thriving and flowering. You will buy into all of the toxicity. You will feel like a failure of a plant.

You might be struggling alone in the middle of the desert, while others are in a botanical garden with constant care. Yet, others will still judge you for not flowering like the others. It's crazy, I know. But this is how people are. They judge very quickly, and without considering all of the circumstances. Then you buy into their judgements, and take them on as fact, even though they are all lies and not an accurate depiction of the truth and reality of your full situation.

Stop buying into the garbage. You do not deserve to be judged.

You most certainly do not deserve to be judged through false and flawed perceptions.

Now let us go back to the initial assertion again. Others look at you in disappointment. You see this, or you feel this. What will you do? Will you buy into it? Will you own their judgments? Will you internalize their opinions of you?

No. You will stop. You will think. You will remind yourself that their perceptions of you are based upon only a slice of evidence, along with their limited view of your full circumstances and situation. Thus, their opinion is already invalid and garbage.

But what's more, is that you will remind yourself that they are trying to accuse you of your entire struggle in life as being your fault. They don't take into consideration that you might be a plant trying to grow without good soil, water, or sunlight. You might be trying to grow without love. Without love from those judging you, I might add. Toxic. They are toxic.

How can a plant grow with toxin being poured onto it constantly? It can't. And yet, they will blame you for not growing. Do you know what that is called? It's called gaslighting. When someone does something to you that hurts you, but then blames you for what they have done to you, it's called gaslighting.

People pour toxin on you. Then they accuse you of not growing. They poisoned you, and you struggle to grow. Whose fault is that? They are toxic.

Do not allow it. Do not take it on board. Do not buy into it. Do not own it. Let them keep their false perceptions of you, if they insist. Let them keep their toxin. Remind yourself of everything I have said.

You can focus on making better choices in the future, which is where all of your focus should be. But accepting the misplaced judgments of others is toxic and harmful. Don't accept them.

Others are disappointed in you. Or you FEEL that others are disappointed in you. It sucks either way. It doesn't feel good. But. Who cares? They know nothing. They make uninformed accusatory judgments of blame that are toxic. No thanks.

It is time to heal further by not accepting toxicity from others. Healing in this case is a process of separating out any of your mistakes and bad choices, from the judgements of others. Meaning, you still need to acknowledge our own bad choices, BUT you need to no longer accept or consider the judgements of others. Can you do that? This is what you need to work on.

By no longer accepting and owning the judgements of others, you are removing the toxicity and poison from your own past choices that may have been poor choices. Once the poison is out of your past choices, it allows you to effectively, safely, calmly, and gently, look back on your past choices and learn from any mistakes.

Everyone makes mistakes. You ARE going to make bad choices in life. Everyone does. It is part of being human. It's okay. Your mission is to examine those bad choices, learn from them, and not keep repeating them. You must become good at doing this.

But it's much harder to do, if not impossible, when the process is full of toxicity from the judgment of others. This is why we remove all judgement from others. Have I beaten this subject to death yet? It's important, though.

All of this takes a lot of practice. Whenever someone judges us, or we feel people are disappointed in us, we have a natural trauma response to it. It makes us upset, depressed, and react in very poor ways.

Eliminating this toxic judgement and perceived disappointment that others may or may not have in us, is a necessary skill in being able to survive life.

CHAPTER TEN

Me, Myself, And I

I am alone a lot, but I am not lonely. I know many share this same sentiment. Others do not. But being comfortable in your own company is critical to your independence and emotional health. Relying on others to keep you entertained, or from being lonely, only creates a dependence that keeps you from being an independent fully empowered person.

Are you comfortable in your own company? If not, why not? Are you just not used to being alone, or is there something about being alone with yourself that you don't like? Would you go out on a date with yourself? If not, why not?

I know everyone is different. Some people are truly social creatures, and I think that is fine. But even so, it is healthy to be comfortable alone also. Others of us could live alone on a deserted island, and be perfectly content, and perhaps never want to leave. Different strokes for different folks.

Personally, I rarely feel alone because I have the constant company of Me, Myself, and I. It's the three of us. We get along pretty well most of the time, although sometimes I get annoyed with Myself, but liking Myself is something I should always do. So, all of us can sometimes scuffle, but usually it works out pretty well.

I am not just being cheeky. When I am alone, I often do think of being in the company of myself, as if I were a small group of close friends. You can think of me as crazy if you want, but I do what works. And yes, I talk to Myself as well, especially when nobody is around to talk with Me. The two of them talk a lot.

Oh, now I can't stop. My apologies. Seriously though, I am often very busy within my own thoughts with myself. I usually have plenty to think about and consider. I also know what I enjoy and what I dislike. I know myself. And while I have plenty of weaknesses and things that I wish were different about myself, all in all I am very content with who I am.

Are you comfortable with who you are? If not, why not? It could be that you are totally fine with yourself and who you are, but you just do not like being alone. That's fine. My only point is that a well-balanced person should be able to feel comfortable alone with themselves. If you are not, then it might be something to examine, consider, and work on.

My suggestion is to use the concept of "Me, Myself, and I." This concept allows you to feel like you are never alone because you always have the ample company of yourself. Perhaps Me, Myself, I, and Yourself, make four? It's starting to get crowded in here now.

If you typically are not comfortable alone, start thinking about what you might enjoy about your own company. Start to embrace those qualities. You will begin to see that I am up to much more than just helping you become more comfortable alone. I am also urging you to explore and recognize more facets of yourself.

Spending time alone, and thinking about how you feel about that, is an excellent excuse and opportunity for some self-exploration and inner work. If there are things that bug you about yourself, maybe that is a prompt to make some minor adjustments. If you love other things about yourself, maybe that is a prompt to bring those traits more out into the open for all to see.

Doing this type of self-work is a great opportunity to foster self-improvement, as well as raise your own self-esteem once you realize how great you are to hang out with, even if it is by yourself.

Next time you are alone, perhaps give some consideration to all I have said, and ask yourself some questions. Then listen for the answers. You might learn something. At the very least, you will have engaged in some meaningful discussions with yourself that did not involve being dependent on the company of others.

CHAPTER ELEVEN

Soul Family

This chapter is for those who struggle with their genetic family, or no longer have one. If you have the perfect genetic family, that is wonderful, and you are blessed. You may move forward without paying a toll. But for the rest of us, this is a necessary chapter.

Stop trying to force a square peg into a round hole. For some people, much of their suffering results from bad feelings regarding family relations. Maybe you and your family do not get along. Maybe you do not feel loved and accepted within your family. What do you do in response to this? Most people respond by trying harder. People want so badly to be loved, accepted, and supported by their family. Even if they are not, they will make excuses as to why this might be.

People will blame certain events, certain people, or blame themselves. Humans are always trying to find and place blame. People think that maybe if a certain person will open their heart and mind, they will see the err in their ways and will start loving them.

Other people think that if they are more patient, try harder, and try for a longer period of time, that maybe they can "win" or "earn" the love and acceptance of their family. Very often, there is always a "helpful" (translated as "totally non-helpful and toxic") family member who will tell you exactly why things are *your* fault. You might believe them. Even if you say you do not believe them, your soul might feel the pain of this inside, to the point of believing them.

All of this is toxic. It is hard to get through a chapter in this book without at least alluding to toxicity. You will also realize, if you have not already, that a major key to surviving life, is removing toxicity from your life as much as possible.

This is one of several chapters where some people may disagree with my approach. That is completely fine. If you have different beliefs that dictate handling toxic families differently than I am suggesting, you are free to ignore my approach and do things your way. Everyone needs to do what is best for them in their unique situation. However, I am going to offer my approach for those who might find it useful, or for others who might be inspired to take some of my ideas and apply them to their own approach.

The bottom line to my approach in dealing with toxic families is to stop trying to pound that square peg into the round hole. Just stop. I won't even use the phrase "give up." I'll just use the phrase, "just stop." Life is too short to be trying to force things that don't want to fit.

I am not saying that you have to stop seeing your family, or that you have to stop loving your family. I am just suggesting that you come to a place of acceptance where you acknowledge to yourself that you and your family might not resonate with each other, and the pieces do not fit.

More importantly, I am suggesting that some detachment is totally necessary if there is toxicity involved. If your family situation is so toxic that it is damaging your self-esteem or mental health, then you must detach out of self-preservation.

If you have determined by now that your genetic family situation is not working, and is likely not going to work, then we will move forward at this point with the alternative plan. That plan is what I call "the soul family." A soul family is a collection of people you "collect" while going through life, that you resonate with, and they end up becoming your family.

Plenty of people already have this to a degree. They might have made close friends that act as their brothers and sisters. That part is common and easier. But what I am suggesting is having a purposeful intention of completely filling out your life with all of the family positions. What I mean by this is seeking out people to fill the roles of mom, dad, uncles, grandparents, siblings, and so forth. It is not that I am trying to replace everyone in your genetic family, but hmmm, I am kind of suggesting that maybe you are. But I am not doing this out of hate or lack of love for your genetic family. You can still love them as your genetic family. But if that family structure is not working for you, I am suggesting that you can build a SECOND family, which is the soul family. In essence, you would end up with two different families, consisting of a genetic family and a soul family.

Someone might ask, "Why go through all of this?" "Why not just learn to deal with your genetic family, or adjust to not having any family at all?"

My answer to those questions, and my personal opinion about it, is that some sort of family support system is very helpful, if not necessary, in trying to survive life. I am not saying that a person can't get through life alone. They certainly can, and some of us have done that to a certain degree. But nobody is an island all of the time, and at certain points in your life, you will need a support system, at least temporarily.

Your soul family can become a great support system when your genetic family is not up to the task. My experience has been that a strong support system is imperative in thriving through life. Setbacks and traumas are going to happen in your life whether you want to think about it or not. When they do, it is very helpful to have others to lean on. Sometimes we need a shoulder to cry on, or a pair of ears to listen to us, or some arms to hug us. Sometimes we might need more concrete help like help with transportation, logistics, housing, or financial. Basically, we all need something at some point, but we don't all have a genetic family willing to give us what we need.

The big important task, of course, is the small (not so small) matter of finding your soul family. This is not easy, nor should it be. Soul families should be earned positions. They are earned by you showing a willingness to be there for them, and them wanting to reciprocate. There is not always a match. Many friends are only willing to take. Conversely, YOU cannot be one of those friends just looking to take. Building a soul family is more about you offering yourself to others, more than it is trying to see who will give to you.

I truly believe that the best way to seek out soul family members is by you making the first move and giving of yourself to people whom you think are good candidates. THEN, after you have given, you can see if that candidate seems willing to give back.

A soul family is a complicated arrangement. It is not about giving to others out of charity, in which you don't expect anything in return. But it is also not strictly a business arrangement of mutual benefit. A soul family is lost somewhere in the middle of those things. You must be willing to give of yourself without any immediate or arranged recompense. But at the same time, you must be able to receive the support from that person when it is truly needed by you. Basically, it needs to be structured as a healthy friendship would be structured. Each person gives because they want to give, not because they demand something in return. BUT, each person also realizes that it only works when both people give to each

71

other. This is a healthy relationship.

I have noticed, and experienced myself, that when genetic family relationships break down, it is often because the relationship became toxic due to an imbalance. Sometimes, family will give more than their share, and then they become bitter about what they gave. As result they will completely cut the person off as a way of compensating for over-giving. Conversely, some family members might give willingly, but then the other member never gives in return, even though they have the ability to give in return. That is a key phrase by the way. "Even though they have the ability to give in return." If a family member has no ability to give in return, some grace needs to be extended. But if a family member IS ABLE to give in return, but they don't, then that creates an imbalance. I mention all of this because you want to be careful that your soul family does not turn toxic like your genetic family may have done. Let us not repeat past mistakes, yes?

Your motto should be, "I will take when I absolutely need to, and I will give generously and freely when I am able." If everyone lives by that motto, there shouldn't be a problem. It is definitely on the honor system, and all parties need to feel comfortable that everyone is playing fairly.

Getting back to the business of finding your soul family, and filling those vacant positions, we can assume that you likely understand how to fill the positions of brothers and sisters. Those are your good friends who grow into your soul family. Much more interesting is seeking out the positions of your parents, "mom and dad," "elders," "mentors," or however you want to phrase it and call them.

More often than not, you are seeking parental figures who perhaps are looking for the same arrangement as you are. Maybe they don't fully realize they are seeking such a formal arrangement, but in their heart, they are seeking that. Maybe they never had kids, or maybe their kids live far away, or it could be that they are estranged from their kids and have no functioning genetic family, similar to your situation.

Let me say this up front. It is my belief that just because one child discarded their parent "for cause," does not mean that you cannot have a perfectly healthy relationship with that same parent. Sometimes people simply do not resonate with each other, or there are past events and traumas that both parent and child were unable to resolve. In other words, you may find a perfectly nice parental figure, whose child is estranged from them because the child thinks their parent is toxic. But you might find that parental figure to not be toxic to you at all. The dynamics of the personalities between you and them might mean that no toxicity exists, even though it might exist in the other relationship the parent has with their genetic child.

The same is true with a potential soul child. The parent of that child might claim that the child is totally toxic, but you find the child to be anything but toxic. It could be that the child's parent is lying, or that the child's parent is the toxic one, OR more than likely it is because that relationship between the two truly is toxic just because of the dynamics of those two specifically, but your relationship with the child is completely nontoxic. Of course, when I say "child" I am likely referring to an adult who you will look upon as your soul child, just as they look upon you as their soul parent.

So, forget about what that person's family says about them. Focus on how that candidate acts around *you* and treats *you*. Your relationship with them will likely be completely different than the relationship they have in the genetic family.

When seeking out older soul family members, such as parents or grandparents, I find it most practical that the younger person be the one to reach out first. Older people often assume that younger people will have no interest in them, and they will not bother to reach out for fear of being annoying and being rejected.

The younger person needs to reach out to the older person first. It is easy to do. Make a pleasant gesture of holding a door, picking something up, asking if they need help with what they are doing, or giving a compliment. See how they respond. They might be mean and have no interest. OR they may respond in a very pleasant way because they might be yearning for social human contact. You can then start a conversation with them.

It's sort of like dating, except without the romantic sexual complications and expectations that come from that awkward mess. So, like with dating, try to find something you might have in common with them. Perhaps you see they have a dog. Maybe ask if they know of a good place to walk their dog, and maybe suggest you meet them there sometime if they would like company to walk their dog with. Always be safe and respectful in your suggestions. Older people are often afraid they are being scammed or taken advantage of. So be gentle.

The point is to seem very friendly and kind toward the older person. Most older folks respond very well to gentle kindness. If they are lonely, they will be open to meeting in a safe place if the proposition does not sound too weird.

During your conversations, or subsequent conversations, act how you want the relationship to look like. For example, if you are looking for a soul parent or grandparent, treat them that way. Ask them for advice. Listen carefully and respectfully to their answers. Offer them help for any tasks they may need help with. You are not just interviewing them for the position of soul parent or soul grandparent, but you are also applying for the job as their soul child.

So, you need to show that you are a respectful and helpful soul child.

If I have not been clear enough, the above tactic is relevant for seeking out both parents *and* grandparents. All it requires is you intentionally making social contact with older people who you have a good feeling about. Sometimes it will work and sometimes it won't. But I promise you will have some wonderful experiences on the journey, and at the very least, make some new friends, even if it does not turn out to be a permanent soul family arrangement.

Notice what we have done here. We made an assessment of our current genetic family situation. If the square peg will never fit into the round hole, we quietly and gently detach and distance from the toxicity. Removing the toxicity from our lives should have already improved your life. But then we became more social toward those who we get a good vibe from and want to see if they might work as a soul family member. We meet new people. We meet new friends. Sometimes we get lucky and find that soul family member we were seeking. But whatever ends up happening, you find yourself living a healthier and more meaningful life through your human interactions.

If your family doesn't fit for you, or you have no family at all, don't give up. You don't have to be alone. You can have a family. Not only that, but sometimes a soul family is the best kind of family. Go out there and find them. Find your people. I promise that your people, your soul family, is out there somewhere, and they are likely looking for you as well.

CHAPTER TWELVE

When Others Reject You

We all hate being rejected. When a person is rejected, their first thought is usually, "What is wrong with me?" That is the absolute worst thought to have, because it is not an accurate picture of what is going on, in addition to the fact that it is damaging to your self-esteem.

So, if there is nothing wrong with you, then why would another person reject you? There are a variety of possibilities. Let us look at a couple of them.

There might be something about you that triggers them into a negative space. You might be "too much" for them. Perhaps you seem too confident for them. Perhaps you are too dominant in their eyes. Maybe they feel you are superior to them. Whatever it is, they can't handle you. But this is not your fault or your problem. This is their own shortcoming that they cannot handle you for one reason or another.

Therefore, they may reject you not because there is something wrong with you, but because there is something wrong with them. They may be inferior or weaker in a certain area and interacting with you makes them feel bad about themselves, or it triggers them into remembering difficult interactions they had with another person who had your traits. None of this is your fault, and there isn't much you can do about it.

Another common reason for someone rejecting another, might be that your energy does not resonate with them. Some people might even say this out loud. If they do say this out loud, you would likely take it as an insult. But it's not an insult. It is just a statement of fact from their point of view.

Does it matter to you if a person says that your energy does not resonate with them, or if you say that THEIR energy does not resonate with YOU? Would you feel better if it was you rejecting them, instead of them rejecting you? If it makes a difference to you, then this means your ego is heavily involved. The truth is that the end-result is the same, whether they say or think it, or you think it or say it. The truth is the truth. Sometimes people do not resonate with each other. There is nothing wrong with this. We have to start normalizing the reality that different people have different energy, and sometimes the energies of two people do not resonate with each other. This concept is nothing new, but it has traditionally been viewed as more of an insult and carries a negative connotation. Instead, we need to view it as a healthy recognition of a healthy or unhealthy combination between two people.

If someone is not comfortable with your energy, they will reject you. That's fine. It is very possible that if they do not resonate with your energy, you might not resonate with them once you got to know them better. So, it is better for both people to just "skip it," and move on.

So far, we have talked about people rejecting you because you made them feel a certain way, in a negative way. Now let's talk about the flip side of that. Believe it or not, there will be some people who reject you because you resonate with them too strongly. This often happens within a romantic dating situation. If a person has come out of a relationship, and is afraid to enter into another one, they may reject you if they feel you are "too perfect," and they will fall in love with you too quickly. The funny thing is that if they could see up front that you are not a match, they are more likely to hang out with you for a while. But if they see you are a perfect match and they are already having feelings for you, they might run for the hills as fast as they can, in order to avoid falling in love again too quickly. They are clearly not ready to start dating yet.

I have also seen in dating situations, where one person is toxic and only into dating for the "thrill of the chase." They will reject you once "the chase" is over. They might really like you, but for them the entire fun of the whole thing was about the "chase" and the mystery. It is exciting for them, and that is why they are dating. They are not looking for an actual healthy relationship. They just want to date for a recreational activity for entertainment purposes. Once they feel the relationship is starting to become firm and strong, they will reject you in order to get out of the relationship, so that they can start the game over again with someone else.

People also reject you because they feel intimidated by you. They are clearly not an intellectual match for you. Again, this does not have anything to do with something being wrong with you. It has more to do with the other person's inability to cope with someone 'intimidating' like you.

I hope you are starting to see the trend here. Most of the time when a person rejects you, it has more to do with them than it does you. This reality means that you should change how you respond to

78

rejection. Instead of taking rejection as a horrible invalidation of you as a person, you should take rejection as a sign that there is something about the other person that prevents them from properly resonating with you.

If anything, you can feel sorry for the other person. They likely have some kind of emotional or mental issue that prevents them from properly relating to other people. It's not just you, but rather they likely have issues with many other people as well. Stop having a trauma response when someone rejects you. Instead, look at them as if something is wrong with *them*. The 'clash' might be perfectly innocent, such as an incompatibility with your energies, or it might be something more dysfunctional like them being unable to handle your personality. Whatever the reason, you cannot allow rejection to put you into a trauma response.

'Surviving Life' means accepting the fact that not everyone can handle you, and not everyone will like you. These things are not your fault.

Just keep being you!

CHAPTER THIRTEEN

The Heart Aches

The heart aches

The heart aches to be loved

It aches to be understood

It aches to be heard

The heart wants to express itself

The heart wants to be creative

It wants to be accepted

It wants to be included

The heart cries when broken

The heart wants to be held

It wants to be soothed

It wants to be healed

The heart screams in pain

The heart cries for help

The heart needs

The heart needs what it needs

Why does nobody understand this?

Why does nobody understand the heart?

Why does nobody want to help heal it?

Why does the heart always want to cry?

The heart beats with the pain of humanity

Your humanity

Your humanity just wants to be human

Why is that so painful?

Humanity is the experience of being human

But what is that?

Humanity is the experience of the need for love

Why is that so painful?

The need for love is so painful

The need for love is so euphoric

The lacking is a depth of loneliness for which no words exist

The feeling of absolute love is a high for which no words exist

The chase for love consumes us and exhausts us

The rejection shatters us

To not feel worthy of it breaks us

The pain can kill us

But the chase and the rejection are the loving lesson

The cruelty of it all is trying to teach us

But we don't listen

We only cry

There is a cure

There is a lesson to be learned

We cannot chase love

We cannot capture love

We can only be love

We can only BE love

We cannot lose what we already are

We cannot be rejected from what we already are

Do not try to stay in the house of love for only minutes

Move into the house of love to live there

If you are love, then you live love

Nobody can take from you what you are

You do not have love

You are not given love

Those can be taken away

Instead, you are love

How?

Such lofty words with no practical way?

Are you lost?

Do you need help?

Think of what makes your heart ache

What makes it scream for help?

What makes it cry?

What do you need most?

WHAT DO YOU NEED MOST?

Love, Understanding, Expression

So, BE them

Be them to everyone, and to yourself

Don't ask. Don't chase.

Just BE

Be the embodiment of what you need

BE the embodiment of what you NEED

Listen, Hear, Understand, Allow Expression, Love

Be this for others

Be this for yourself

Become what you need most

Allow yourself full expression

Allow yourself to be heard

Fully understand yourself

Fully accept yourself

Fully love

Your heart may still cry when hurt

But those cries will be cries of expression

They will not be cries of lacking

Deep within your soul, you will know you are loved

You will know that you are what you need most

You will be the best of humanity

You will be love

Brian Hunter 2022

CHAPTER FOURTEEN

Why Are So Many People Mean?

This is the kind of chapter that gets me into trouble. Some people will accuse me of being negative by phrasing the chapter title the way I did. People will say, "Why don't you talk about all of the nice people in the world instead?" All of the Law of Attraction people will say, "You should phrase it the other way around in order to create the reality you want to create."

Yeah, I get it. First of all, I don't believe in the Law of Attraction. I believe that bad things happen to good people, regardless of their positive thoughts, intentions, and actions. So there is that. But secondly, I can work to create a better reality while still phrasing the chapter title the way I phrased it. Finally, I phrased it the way I did because that is what most people are thinking and wondering, at least some of the time. Most people are thinking, "Why is everyone so mean these days?" But you see, I actually toned it down and made it less accusatory and biting, by how I phrased it. You're welcome. My pleasure. Anything to make the world more pleasant.

Now let's get on with business. Why ARE people so mean? And I am not talking about a ten-year-old brother and sister being mean to each other. I am not talking about your ex being mean to you. I am not talking about your mother-in-law being mean to you. I am actually talking about complete strangers, and those only loosely associated with you. It just seems that so many people out in the general public can be very mean, and randomly reactive.

There are also lots of people who are wonderful and nice. In fact, more than half of the people in the world are wonderful and nice. Yes, I am admitting to a majority being nice. I LOVE some of the people out there. They are wonderful! But they are not the problem. We need to focus on the problem. So, let us look at the people who are mean for seemingly no reason whatsoever.

The reason I am discussing this subject is because dealing with random mean people can be very triggering for many people. Plenty of people have a trauma response when someone is mean to them, even if it is a stranger, and ESPECIALLY if it is a stranger. Why is this?

Well, many of us carry trauma with us from our childhood or past relationships when our family or partner was very mean to us. It could have been outright abuse, or it could have been more emotional passive-aggressive type behavior. Regardless of the exact form of the abuse, we are traumatized from the abuse. It likely caused us to carry feelings of instability, as well as a damaged self-esteem. Any way you slice it, the "meanness" from our past was very toxic, and the toxicity made us sick. It traumatized us, and it made it so that we are immediately triggered when someone, even a stranger, is mean to us for no reason.

A stranger might be mean, and we see our parent in that person, or we see our abusive ex-partner. It could be anyone, but we immediately are pulled back into whatever old abusive relationship or situation we used to be in, or are still presently stuck in.

Once we are triggered by the person being mean to us, we are in our trauma response mode, which usually means we get anxiety, maybe even panic, and likely depression. It's not fun. It ruins our day. It makes it difficult to "survive life."

So, what is our goal in examining this topic? Our goal is to reduce and minimize the amount of triggering and trauma we experience through our interactions with random, or not so random, mean people. If we can learn to do this, then life will become a little easier, yes?

Okay then. The absolute first thing we must learn to do is to see the "mean" interaction for what it is. Any situation is less traumatizing once you reduce it to something simpler and smaller. Therefore, let us look at a mean interaction for what it really is.

Whenever a person is mean to you, it is almost never about you. Maybe read that last line again. Realize that people are almost never mean specifically because of you. You were only the convenient excuse and trigger for them to be mean. You were likely in the wrong place at the wrong time, doing the wrong thing. You triggered them, just like they then triggered you.

People who are mean are usually this way for a few potential reasons, and we will go over those possibilities. First, they might be mean because that is how they were raised, and that is the culture in which they live. If they had meanness around them, or have meanness around them presently, then they will be a product of their environment. With these folks, they are not being mean in order to hurt you. Rather, they are being mean to you because that is how they treat everyone. To them it is normal acceptable behavior. They don't think they are being mean.

Another possible reason they are mean is because they possess no empathy. People with no empathy have no inhibitions about being mean. They simply don't care. They have no concept of the trauma they are causing you, nor do they care. They are just machines doing what they do. Until something in their life causes them to find, or realize, empathy, they will always act the way they do, which is often mean. Being mean is a habit for such people.

The third and most common reason people are mean, is that they themselves have been victims of trauma at the hands of mean people, or by life circumstances. This is similar to how most abusers were abused themselves at some point in the past.

If a person suffers in life, they often become mean. This is another reason we are discussing all of this. If you are suffering in life, we do not want you to become mean because of it. When people suffer, usually one of two things happen. Either they become even more empathetic, OR they turn off their emotions and their empathy as a coping mechanism. If a person turns off their emotions and empathy, they will become mean.

For example, let us say that some random older man has suffered some losses in his life, got treated like crap by his father, was treated like crap by his boss, lost his job after years of loyalty, and he just had a bad time of it in general. He was basically abused by life, and thus was traumatized. If this man is angry and bitter from what happened to him in his life, he will often carry this anger with him everywhere he goes. So, if you get in his way at the grocery store, he will use that as an excuse to vent his anger and lash out at you.

Is the man really that angry with *YOU*? No. You only got in his way. It's not a big deal. Even he probably doesn't care that you got in his way. But he was already so incredibly annoyed by his own life experience, that it triggered him into lashing out. In response, he will be mean to you.

Then, him being mean to you, will trigger you into your trauma response. You will feel terrible. You might even think that it was your fault that you got in the man's way. You will be reminded about how your parent or partner used to yell at you the same way for getting in *their* way. This trigger of your trauma will plunge you into depression, panic, or anxiety. Your day will be ruined. People have been known to come home from the grocery store and cry because a random man in the store yelled at them.

We have to short-circuit this sequence of events. We have to prevent your trauma response from activating due to the mean person, and most certainly prevent any meltdown that might follow.

So, here is how this needs to go from now on. First of all, before you go out in public, remind yourself that you could have an interaction with a mean person at any time. You might also run into really nice people. But the point is that you need to remain mentally prepared, so that you are less likely to be traumatized by surprise if you encounter a mean person.

This way, when you are in the grocery store and the mean man yells at you, you will have been prepared for this possible interaction. You will look at the situation for what it is. Instead of immediately going into a trauma response, you will remain detached and recognize that you only got in the man's way. You didn't do anything wrong of any significance.

Next, is the most important step. You will remind yourself that he is not angry at you. It's not about you. He is mean because he carries anger, pain, or abuse from his own life. He is only venting. You are the unfortunate soul at the wrong place at the wrong time. Don't worry, he yells at everyone in his life. You are just one of his many victims that week.

You must remain calm and keep reminding yourself of his own miserable existence, and his anger issues. I look at people like this as "things." I just stare at them and wonder what they will do or say next. I don't take in anything they say. I do not allow their venom to enter my being. My hair might be standing on end, but I will remain calm inside, and I certainly will not respond to them. I just look at them, and work on remaining calm.

Once the initial shock is gone, I keep reminding myself of how they are just miserable in their life, and I keep telling myself that it was not about me. It is always about them. They require excuses to vent their own anger and pain for their own reasons, having nothing to do with me.

This is all easier said than done. It takes practice. But you need to develop this skill. You cannot allow people like this to put you into a trauma response. You cannot allow "outside people" to control your emotions.

I should also mention that your response to mean people will be the same, regardless of *why* they are mean. For example, if the person is mean because they have zero empathy, the response is the same. In fact, the response is even more important, and easier to deal with. A person with no empathy is basically just a machine. Look at them that way. Think of them as a machine. People without empathy are missing part of their humanity, so they are indeed part machine. Do not take what they say personally, much as how you would handle dealing with a robot that says something insulting to you. You would just stare, then ignore, and walk away.

Mean people who became that way from being raised that way, or because it's part of their culture, can be a little more dangerous. Some of these folks can be psychotic because they think their behavior is normal and acceptable. This is why it is even more important to never respond. You want to detach from the situation as quickly as possible and walk away. Think of these people as a very scary barking dog. You want to remain as far from the scary dog as possible so that it won't bite you.

So, in summary, why are some people mean? It is not because of you. It is because of them. It is their own issues causing them to be mean, not you. If society continues to be a more difficult place to live and survive in, you can expect more people to become mean. With that said, let's not add to the pile of meanness. If you are one of the people who is carrying anger from past abuse and trauma, it is important that you are cognizant of the potential for you to become one of the mean people lashing out. Please don't.

If you are carrying anger and pain, try to release it through your own self-work, therapy, exercise, time in nature, or whatever works for you. Experiencing trauma is an unwanted life experience, but it can also make us feel more empathy for others who are in pain. Instead of trauma making you a worse person, allow it to make you a better person. Turning trauma and disadvantage into a tool for personal betterment is a key concept and skill in becoming a more powerful person, and surviving life.

CHAPTER FIFTEEN

If I Saw You sitting On A Park Bench

Picture yourself sitting alone on a park bench. If I came walking along, and noticed you sitting there alone, would you want me to sit with you? Would that be too creepy and weird?

First of all, why are you sitting on a park bench all alone? Are you just enjoying being outside? Are you lonely and wanting to be outside with others walking by? Or do you hate people, and you just want to be left alone in peace while you relax?

Let us assume that you are not waiting for anyone, and my intentions are not romantic or weird in any way. Let's say that like you, I was out for a walk, enjoying nature, and I was used to walking alone. However, I saw you sitting alone on the bench, and there was something about your energy that intrigued me.

Perhaps you seemed interesting or nice to me in some way. How can I tell this from you only sitting silently on a bench? Well, I guess you don't know me well, do you? Let's just say I can tell plenty about people just by observing them for a few seconds, and I will leave it at that for now.

I sit down on the other end of the bench. I pretend not to be too weird, and I don't try to look at you, or cause you to want to run for your life quite yet. I enjoy the same view that you have been enjoying. You picked a nice bench. It has a great view of the park and all of the trees, but it also a great view of all of the people walking by. It's a perfect spot for people-watching and enjoying the nice day.

I wonder to myself how long I am going to sit there and pretend that you are not sitting on the other end of the bench. You are likely wondering how long I will sit there before I go away and leave you the entire bench to yourself again.

Why are you feeling this way? Does my presence bother you? You seem tense. Even if you are not freaked out by me, you seem tense that I am sitting on the same bench as you. Why is that? Are you not used to human contact? Or is it just that I am a stranger? You don't even know who I am or what I do. For all you know, I might be an author who writes tons of interesting books. Why automatically assume that I am just an annoying weird stranger?

Perhaps I finally get sick of sitting there and pretending that you are not there near me. After all, I initially sat down on your bench because I sensed something interesting about you. I look over at you, and say, "It's really nice here, isn't it?"

What are you thinking? Are you thinking, "Oh here we go! This guy is now going to try and talk to me, ugh." Or are you going to think, "It's about time he said something." I bet it's the first one, isn't it?

Let's pretend that you respond, "Yeah, it's a nice day and a pleasant park." Well, that doesn't give me much to work with, now does it. I will figure you are trying to be polite, but likely hate talking to strangers.

But I'm not your average bear. I am an author and do counseling work, so I am no stranger to communication sparring. So, I am going to up the ante and ask you a question that requires a real answer. I am going to say to you, "How does this place make you feel?"

At this point, I have thrown down the gauntlet. You are either going to get up and walk away at this point, or you are going to have to answer my question in a meaningful way. Which would you do?

Never mind, don't answer that. I'm not done having my fun yet. Let's say you decide to stay and answer me. How would you answer me? How does sitting on that bench in that park make you feel? Could you answer me honestly and precisely? Would you answer me honestly, or are you only honest with people you know?

Maybe you tell me that sitting there makes you think about your life. That's a fair answer. It's a meaningful answer, without giving me much information about yourself. Nicely played.

However, I'm sorry, but I am always one step ahead of you. I'm not bragging. It's more of a curse actually. But I can tell from your answer and your tone of voice that you are in a contemplative mood, and I sense some pain from your soul. And yes, I can sense pain from your soul just from that limited exchange we just had.

I will continue to escalate the dialogue by saying, "This place really speaks to my soul. It doesn't matter if I am feeling happy or sad. Being here speaks to my soul." I will pause, and then I will say to you, "What does *your* soul say when sitting in this place?"

You will look over at me with a weird look because by this time you have fully realized that I am 'different.' But I'm still not scary enough for you to grab your pepper spray, or for you to get up and leave.

How would you answer my question? What is your soul saying? Do you even know what your soul is saying? I hope you do. You should always listen to your soul, even if it is just whispering things.

Your soul speaks your truth.

At this point in the conversation, you have to decide whether to just keep being polite, or whether to be totally honest. Perhaps you cannot decide at first. You kind of want to be honest with me. I seem to be asking interesting questions, and I seem to be willing to listen. But you still have your doubts because I am a stranger and we are not supposed to bare our souls to strangers, right?

You decide to be honest, without giving away your bankcard pin codes to this stranger. You might say, "I have been going through some stuff lately, so my soul is thinking. My soul doesn't know what to say. It's just thinking about what to do."

Good answer. Impressive even. It shows you have depth, but I still have no idea what you are talking about. But don't get over-confident. I know how to play this game.

I respond, "Yeah, I know what you mean. I can't even tell you how many times I have been in this park, and my soul has been thinking and screaming in pain from life. But yet, I can come here and find peace as well."

I pause, and then say, "What hurts you?"

I've got you cornered now. You either need to answer my question, or outright refuse. There is no in between.

What would you do? What would you say?

What hurts you?

I am not going to put words in your mouth anymore. It would be disrespectful. But maybe you tell me. You tell me in a polite and direct way, giving me the short version. I listen. I don't reply right away. I take in what you just said.

If I felt you were not going to add to your remarks, I might respond. I would say something about how I can understand what you said, or how I can relate to it in some way. Or perhaps I can't relate to it, but I can indicate to you that I understand your feelings which you just described to me.

It is at this point in the conversation that I might have some kind of story, words of encouragement, or words of advice. If I start giving unsolicited advice, I risk you being annoyed with me, or maybe you will just be wondering who in the world I am, and what I am doing there.

Good question. What AM I doing there? Was I just out for a walk and randomly sat down next to you? Or was I an angel of sorts, who knew you needed to talk about something? Which would you think? Does it matter which it is?

Our little discussion caused you to think and feel about what your soul was thinking and feeling. You then expressed your truth to me. I listened. You were heard. We had a meaningful exchange. I might have even said something intelligent and helpful, but that is probably just my wishful thinking. Even if I didn't, I most certainly listened to you. That's something anyways.

Now let's say that I knew it was my time to get up and leave. One of the most important skills in life is learning when it is time to stop speaking. Nobody likes it when people talk too long. I am one who is always at risk of talking for too long. I have tried to get better at this and take cues from people on when they have had enough of me. Those of you who know me personally, might notice that I will often talk and talk and talk, and then all of a sudden go completely silent, and almost into a "sleep mode." This is probably because I all of a sudden realized that I was talking too much.

Anyways, I will get up from the bench. I will say, "It has been really amazing and wonderful talking with you. Thank you. It was an honor. I really enjoyed it. I truly hope you feel better. Maybe I will see you again sometime."

I will wait to see if you reciprocate in some way, but I do not expect you to do so. You might be really relieved that I am leaving, or you feel awkward and afraid I am going to ask you out on a date or something. So maybe you just wave to me, or maybe you say a few words to make for a polite departure. To be perfectly honest with you, I don't care how you respond. I really don't. I was not in this for your response, your gratitude, your interest in me, or your validation of our conversation. I was in it for our meaningful exchange in the moment only.

But let's say that you politely acknowledge our conversation and wish me well. I then walk away without looking back. You are left sitting on the bench alone, just as before. How do you feel?

Are you relieved I am gone? Or are you feeling a little lonely now that I am gone? Or do you just feel better that I was there, and then left? Are you glad I sat down and spoke with you?

I am just full of questions, aren't I? Oops, there I go again. More questions. I guess I am just asking you to contemplate whether or not you were happy for the human exchange from the stranger, or would you have preferred that I kept walking and never sat down on your bench in the first place?

For my part, I would be very pleased that I sat down on your bench and spoke with you. The reason why is because it is food for my soul when I can have a meaningful conversation with someone. If the conversation is not meaningful, it is like a dentist visit for me. But if it has meaning, and involves truths of the soul, I love it.

Do you feel better after our conversation, or no? What would you do if you saw me walking in the park again? Would you duck and hide, or would you wave at me?

Would you have a similar exchange with another stranger sometime? Would you ever consider initiating such a conversation with someone sometime? You know how to do it now because you watched me do it.

Not everyone appreciates conversations with a stranger. I respect that, and so should you. But sometimes we might appreciate a conversation with a stranger more than we realize. Sometimes we are lonelier than we realize. Sometimes our soul is in pain, and it helps to have someone to at least listen. It can be nice to have someone willing to listen to our truth, even if they don't know us and it has no bearing on our life.

What is the point of this chapter? There is no point. HA! But there is. If you don't think so, then it's fine to move onto more interesting chapters. But to some, this chapter has plenty of meaning. Sometimes we need someone to talk with. Sometimes we need someone to just listen. We need to express our pain, or truth, or our current thoughts and moods.

It should also not be lost upon you that YOU can be the person that sits down and listens. Maybe next time you see someone alone who looks like they are in thought or pain about something, you might consider sitting down on their bench for a short time to see if there is an exchange to be had or not. If not, then get up and leave them to their peace. But maybe there is an exchange to be had.

To survive life, we sometimes need each other, even if we are strangers to each other. Showing some kindness is an incredible gift you can give to humanity. Listening is a generous gift you can give to anyone, even strangers.

I hope you enjoyed our conversation. I certainly did.

CHAPTER SIXTEEN

The Hand from the Other Realm

One afternoon, I was taking a nap. It is not unusual for me to sleep better, and deeper, during my daytime naps. For those who are not familiar with me, it is not uncommon for me to have very vivid strange dreams. I have dreams of dead people, other dimensions, and all kinds of weird things. Please excuse me while I adjust my tinfoil hat. Just back away slowly without making any sudden movements, and I will likely not make any lurching scary movements toward you. So, no worries.

Anyway, I was deep in my one-hour nap, and I was having one of my very vivid dreams. They are so vivid, that I feel they are real. I know they are real. Other than that, I have no proof and no full scientific explanation. I felt I was in some kind of suspended state of being. I was at rest, at ease, and in a very deep meditative state. I had completely let myself go to the point of being in another reality or dimension.

I had been having a really hard time in life, and I was in a state of frustration, exhaustion, and surrender. During this "state of being," I all of a sudden saw a hand extending itself through the clouds, fog, and mist above me. It was a very familiar hand to me. I knew who the hand belonged to. It was the hand of a young male. I can't tell you who it was, because in this current dimension we are all in, I am not absolutely certain who it was. But in my dream state dimension, I absolutely knew who it was. It was like some kind of soul-brother that I had known forever.

The hand extended toward me, and I knew that all I had to do was grab the hand. I had no fear toward the hand because I knew who it was, and I completely trusted the person, and felt very close to the person, and it was almost emotionally, as if I really missed the person intensely.

Deep down, I knew that I could grab the hand, and that would result in me being pulled into *their* dimension. I fully assumed that it would likely mean that I would not be able to exist in my present reality anymore. I suppose it would have meant that I would have died in my present reality.

I WANTED to grab the hand. But I hesitated. I hesitated because I had a few loose ends in my present reality that I could not just leave open-ended. My slight hesitation was all it took for the hand to start receding from me.

The message I received in my mind was that "it" would only work if I had grabbed the hand with complete and total commitment, with zero doubt. If I had done that, I most assuredly would have successfully transferred over to the other dimension.

Still in my dream state, I became frustrated with myself that I did not grab the hand with total commitment. I wanted to leave my present reality. I wanted to go with the hand. But I wasn't ready, I guess. My slight hesitation was my subconscious confirmation that I was not ready, even though I WANTED to be ready.

I watched as the hand completely receded and disappeared into the clouds. It was gone, and I no longer sensed the person whose hand it belonged to. Shortly after the hand disappeared, I woke up.

Upon waking up, I felt certain that what I had just experienced was real. I was also upset and frustrated that I did not take the hand. I regretted hesitating. I wanted to take the hand, and I know it would have been great if I had taken the hand. But I made a choice in the moment. I felt a sense of obligation to stay a little longer and finish up some things.

If I am to be completely honest, the items I did not want to leave undone, were a couple books I was finishing up for my *Living A Meaningful Life* series, and *THIS* book here, *Surviving Life*. How ironic that I did not grab the hand, so that I could stay in my present reality and write a book called *Surviving Life*.

Obviously, sitting here now, I do not regret my choice to stay. Well kind of. But not really. I know my place is here for now. I made the correct choice. I often do what is right, rather than doing what I *want* to do. This was a perfect example of doing what was right, rather than what I wanted.

What do I think of this? What did I learn from this? Well, it confirmed my belief that there are other realms close to ours. I think in the right conditions and state of mind, we can nearly touch those realms, or maybe even completely touch those realms. I am certain that if I had taken the hand, I would not be here right now. Others can say I am crazy and not believe it, and that is totally valid. But I am allowed to believe what I believe, just as you are allowed to do the same.

I think the other important lesson, or reminder, was to be certain of who you are, what you are, what you are doing, what your purpose is, and what your true desires are. If you can't answer all of those things with certainly, then you are likely to feel lost and not be able to make critical choices in critical moments.

I had no fear of leaving. I had no fear of dying. There was no fear. But I knew who I was and what I was doing here in this dimension. I knew of my obligations here, and I knew of my desires to accomplish certain things here. I was certain about it. This caused me to make the critical and instantaneous decision to hesitate to take the hand that I WANTED to take. It caused me to make the CORRECT decision and stay here for now.

There is a lot to consider in what I just said. I have zero doubts about anything I just said. But I invite you to ask yourself if YOU would have any doubts or fears. If you do, I would suggest that you do some contemplating, and resolve any fears or doubts that you would have had.

Having no fears, and having absolute clarity in all things involving yourself, your obligations, and your desires, are all necessary skills in surviving life.

CHAPTER SEVENTEEN

Suicide

I like to talk about the elephant in the room. Sometimes people find me annoying for doing this. That's fine. But I cannot write a book about surviving life without discussing suicide. And I cannot discuss suicide without being totally honest. This means I might make statements, or have opinions, that contradict other things you have heard. I am not saying that I am right about everything. If you have thoughts of suicide, or questions, you should seek professional help. You should go see your doctor. Don't be afraid to seek help. It's okay.

I am going to give you my thoughts on the subject, and you can consider them useful, or not. I could possibly write an entire book on suicide, but for this chapter I am choosing to approach the subject from a different angle. So, realize that I know that suicide is a complex subject with many facets and angles. But I am going to focus on one particular angle that I do not see discussed much.

The traditional line about suicide is that it is a mental illness and that it is a selfish act. I disagree with both of those statements. GASP.

But let me first clarify something. Suicide can come about from different reasons. Some people are quite literally out of their minds when they attempt or commit suicide. They might be under the influence of drugs or other substances. They might have an underlying mental illness that is causing them to have delusions, or extreme acute depression. So yes, suicide can result from mental illness, and often does. But the keyword is CAN. My point was that the traditional view is that suicide IS a mental illness, as if it ALWAYS results from mental illness. I hear people making the statement that "suicide IS a mental illness." I disagree with this.

I believe thinking in those terms dismisses a huge group of people who do not have a traditional underlying mental illness. Instead, what they suffer from is a lack of hope. Is lack of hope a mental illness? Are bad or impossible circumstances a mental illness?

I believe there are a lot of people considering suicide, who are doing so because of horrible circumstances in their lives, and a lack of hope in their lives. That is not a mental illness. And to dismiss these people as "just having a mental illness for which they need treatment," is wrong and not helpful.

If I have horrible circumstances in my life, is that going to be fixed by seeing my doctor? Maybe the doctor will give me some medication to lessen the feelings of my circumstances, but the doctor will not have a pill to fix my circumstances. Reality is reality. Many people these days suffer from the reality of their reality. Their circumstances cause them to suffer, and their circumstances cause them to feel as if there is no hope. This situation can cause thoughts of suicide.

My "suicide equation," which I came up with a while back, states: Suicide = (Intense pain + Lack of hope). Again, I am not talking about suicide that results from delusions or an acute response to an underlying mental illness. I am talking about suicide attempted or committed by otherwise healthy people living a normal life. How sad is it that "normal life," and "healthy people" are now included in the same sentence as the word "suicide?" But that is our reality these days.

Back to the suicide equation. How the equation works is the higher level of "intense pain," and the lower level of "hope" that you have, means the greater chances of suicide. Usually, both elements of the equation have to be "active" for there to be suicide. For example, if a person is experiencing intense pain in their life, but they still maintain hope, that person is not as likely to commit suicide. Additionally, a person can be lacking in hope, but if they are feeling some relief from pain, they are likely to hold off on plans for suicide. The danger zone is when there is a very intense level of pain, along with a feeling of hopelessness. *That* is when suicide occurs.

The way to prevent suicide is to manage the equation effectively. Whether you are trying to help someone else who is suffering and at risk, or you are trying to help yourself, you need to learn to manage the suicide equation. You might even want to write down the equation. Again, it is:

Suicide = (Intense pain + Lack of hope).

We manage this equation by either finding a way to decrease the level of pain, or by increasing the level of hope. Work both variables of the equation at the same time if possible. But even if you can successfully affect only one variable of the equation, that can mean the difference between life and death. Always seek professional help, including emergency help, when and if needed. Also remember that those suffering from severe mental illness or delusions, need immediate professional help. Managing this equation won't work for them.

My point in bringing up this idea of suicide not being a mental illness, is to shine light on the reality that people's current circumstances are often a cause of their suicide. They might seem totally fine to others, and have no history of significant mental illness, other than some level of depression, which a huge majority of people display to some degree these days, at least off and on.

So, for our purposes in this chapter, we are discussing the importance of a person's present circumstances, as it relates to their level of hope. Bad circumstances put a person at risk of suicide. Even if a person does not display erratic behavior, if they are presently suffering from very bad circumstances, then they are at risk of suicide. Trust what I say. Don't dismiss it just because the person seems fine. If they are suffering within their life circumstances, and especially if they seem to see a lack of hope, you had best realize that suicide has likely crossed their mind to a certain level. It's math. That's why I created the equation. I wanted to make it as simple as math, so that people can see it more clearly.

If you or someone you know is struggling with thoughts of suicide, consider both your pain from circumstances, and your level of hope. Realize some things for me please. First of all, EVERYTHING changes eventually. Nothing stays the same. This means that your circumstances WILL CHANGE. I will give you a money back guarantee on that. I can't promise how much they will change, but I can promise that they *will* change. They have to, because everything changes eventually.

Therefore, stop thinking that your life will never change. It will. Thinking your crappy situation will never change is false thinking. You are simply wrong. It will change. When it will change, I do not know. But it will change.

Now a word about hope. Hope is a lot like luck. It can shift within seconds. One moment, there is none, and a minute later, there is an abundance of hope. Realize what I just said. What this means is that if you are having a moment when you think there is no hope, realize that this calculation can change at any moment. You should hold off and wait, just for that reason alone. Let your bad negative moment of "no hope" pass. Sometimes all we need is a walk outside, and we can then realize that while the situation is dire, there is still SOME hope. Your moment thinking that there was "no hope" will pass. So, give hope a chance. Give change a chance. Things will change. And hope springs eternal, however small it might seem at times.

If someone is suicidal, they are not just "mentally ill." They might not be mentally ill at all. They might just be suffering from horrible present circumstances, which is creating intense pain for them, and they are not seeing any hope. Stop accusing people of being mentally ill and dismissing them as just needing "professional help." Lots of times what people NEED are better circumstances, and a reason for hope.

Let's say that again for those in the back not paying attention. Most of the time, what people need most are better circumstances, and a reason for hope.

Some might need to read that previous line again. If you want to prevent suicide, then help someone improve their immediate life circumstances, and give them a reason to have hope. You can do that. Telling them they are mentally ill and need to go get help is not as helpful as you think. In fact, it is not helpful at all to most people. Saying that to them is dismissive of their suffering and is only said by people to alleviate their own guilt and worries over the situation. Maybe try to solve the problem instead of just trying to alleviate your own guilt and worries over the person.

If you are suffering alone, and dealing with all of this alone, you are not the only one. Part of the reason many people consider suicide, is because they feel alone. They might have no support system. A lack of support system contributes to poor circumstances. To all of you who fit into this category, I have this to say.

Consider your circumstances carefully. Never forget that your circumstances will definitely change, since everything changes eventually. But you do not need to just do nothing and wait. Think of ways that you can change your present circumstances immediately. Maybe you will even come up with some ideas by reading this book. Do not be afraid to make drastic life adjustments in an effort to change your present circumstances. It could be a life and death matter, so go ahead and make big changes if you can see the opportunities to do so.

Also, engage in self-care coping mechanisms so that you are more easily able to see hope and decrease pain. Hope is much easier to see while not under a blanket of dark trauma. Self-care helps us see the sunshine a bit more. I mean that literally. Go outside into the sunshine. Things usually seem brighter out in the sunshine. You will begin to see hope again. There is always hope, because things can change at any moment. The fact that things can change at any moment is proof that there is hope. The more likely there is to be change, the more hope you will see.

For this reason, engage in activities that are more likely to cause change. Help yourself out. Do things that increase your level of hope. Even the smallest actions can make a huge difference.

I cannot take away all of your suffering. But maybe I can help you manage it better. Maybe I can provide you with better clarity. I take your suffering seriously. I know for most people; suicide is not some delusional selfish act that is taken lightly. Rather, it is a very serious matter that nobody wants to do, but some feel it is the only way out. I am trying to show you that it is not the only way out. You can manage your equation and find a way through, as everything around you does eventually change.

Please know that you have my love and best wishes in overcoming your personal battles and moving beyond any suffering that you are enduring. I have been there, and I understand. The struggle is real.

For those who wish to read more of my thoughts on the topic of suicide, you can do so in my book *Heal Me*, which features a chapter on the 'Suicide,' plus many other subjects that will help you to overcome life's numerous traumas.

CHAPTER EIGHTEEN

Battling Depression

When I was in college, I was penniless, under-fed, over-tired, somewhat depressed, and a little discouraged. Sometimes when I just couldn't take it anymore, I would stop at the store and buy a big bag of soft chocolate chip cookies. What I didn't eat in the car on the way home, I would eat after I got home. For ten minutes, I felt better. Even after the ten minutes, I felt maybe I could continue on in my life a little longer thanks to the slight moments of relief. I am not sure what would have become of me if I hadn't eaten the bag of chocolate chip cookies when I needed them most.

Sometimes, often times, we find ourselves feeling this way. We feel broken and depleted. If we have been disciplined and lucky enough to not have fallen victim to any serious addictions, we still struggle to rummage forward in life, scraping by for another five minutes.

Sometimes nice people will ask us how we are doing, or if we are okay. Sometimes, family members might ask every once in a blue moon, or more frequently. We might say we are fine (We are not fine). We might know they are just trying to be nice or show

111

concern. But they wouldn't truly understand, nor do they want to truly understand, nor do they have the ability, time, or resources to actually help some of the time. However, if we are lucky, we DO have family or friends who are willing to help. But do we always accept their help? No. That is all part of this mental condition, this mental illness, disease, that we call Depression, with a big "D."

Depression is a serious and important matter. A book about surviving life would not be complete without a chapter on depression. Those of you who have read my book *Heal Me*, will recognize this chapter on depression. This discussion on depression has been so popular in *Heal Me*, that I felt compelled to include it in this book as well.

Some of you may be in a very dark place. Some of you may be surrounded by the darkness of depression. Maybe you cannot stop crying. Maybe you don't want to get out of bed or leave your house. Maybe you see no hope and no way out. Maybe you think your life is over. Maybe you want your life to be over. Nobody can quite understand all of your pain, and there is no way to adequately explain it to others, nor do you have the energy to do so.

It is a heavy weight of darkness that feels like it will never go away. How can anyone have any hope if it will never go away, you might think. You wonder, how can I ever get better if I have no energy to fight?

You just need the pain to stop. I understand, and I hear your cries through the darkness. I know you sometimes feel it's hopeless, but I come offering you hope. Your tears are an expression of your pain, but your human spirit is proof of the light that still awaits you in this life. It is time to get better. Come with me. I will show you the face of your enemy and we will conquer it together.

I describe depression as an insidious crippling monster that can leave you in constant pain. It is a heavy weight of darkness that covers you and cannot be simply washed away. The first step in facing depression is to realize that depression is nothing more than a monster that tells lies. Depression is a monster that lives inside your head, always lurking. It finds all of your deepest and darkest fears, insecurities, traumas, and vulnerabilities. It takes all of the information it gained from accessing these, and it whispers things in your head to trigger you into despair and paralysis. Depression knows exactly what to whisper in order to control your thoughts and keep you in darkness.

Depression wants to kill you. That is its ultimate goal. Depression hopes that if it whispers the right things at the right moments for a long enough period of time, that you will decide to take your life by your own hand, by substance abuse, or any other means. While it works to that end, its intermediate goal is to keep you in as much pain as possible, darkness, paralysis, and hopelessness.

Depression is an abuser. It wants to beat you down and weaken you enough so that it controls you. The control it seeks is to keep you from taking the necessary steps to leave it. Yes, just like an abuser, it does not want you to leave it. It wants to keep enough control over you so that you can't and won't leave. But unlike human abusers, depression rarely makes mistakes, and it never gets tired. For this reason, it is very hard to shake and to leave.

Usually when we examine why you are in pain, we look for what the core issue is that caused it. But in the case of depression, it really does not matter as much what caused it. It can be caused by many things, as you know. Most traumas can cause depression, and most people at some point will experience some level of depression. So with depression, we are not going to focus on the core issue of what caused it, as much as we would with other issues. Instead, we are simply going to focus on getting rid of it. The reason I take this approach is because although the core issues for causing the depression should be addressed, it is nearly impossible to fully address core issues while you are paralyzed and controlled by depression. So really, the depression needs to be brought under control first, before you can think clearly with the strength needed to fully resolve core issues.

The most important thing you should realize, fully accept, and remember, is that depression is a monster in your head that lies. This is critically important because you MUST become very cognizant from now on that everything it whispers in your head is a lie, or twisted in some way. You have to stop taking it seriously, taking it to heart, and even listening, or paying it much attention. You have to call out its whispers as invalid. Like all abusers, depression relies on constant systematic brainwashing to keep you under its control. Thus, you have to break the cycle of abuse.

Let us say you are alone in your thoughts, and all of a sudden you feel that thick black cloud coming over you. You sense the monster is present. Then it whispers something in your head. It whispers one of its common thoughts that it uses to trigger you into depression, anxiety, or panic. The first thing you need to do is think, "Not today, Satan." That is me being tongue and cheek during a dead-serious somber discussion. But in all seriousness, you need to think, "Go away." "I dismiss you." "I am not listening to you today." You can come up with whatever thought works best for you. You have to realize it is just a monster using your inner most "issues" to whisper something that will trigger you into pain and paralysis. It is hoping to control you and eventually make you so despondent that perhaps it can kill you.

So, right there we have called it out on its' bullshit. We know what game it's playing. We know what it is, how it's playing, and what it hopes to accomplish.

114

RESIST.
DO NOT PLAY ALONG.
DISMISS IT.

But beware. The monster is strong, clever, and does not give up easily. It will search and look for other inner issues and fears you have that it can try and use against you. It is trying to trigger you. So, when you dismiss its first attack, you can expect it to make additional attacks in an effort to find something else that will successfully trigger you into despair and keep you under its control. Therefore, be ready to receive these further attacks, and be ready to dismiss them as well.

The trick to all this, which takes practice, is to always expect it to attack and whisper something that you do not want to hear. It will always try and come up with something new, or a different angle on something old. But the one common underlying theme it will always use is HOPELESSNESS.

Remember, it wants to kill you. Therefore, it will try to use the suicide equation against you by increasing pain and stripping you of hope. It will always strive to convince you that your life is hopeless. It will try to convince you that your problems and pain will never go away. You know this feeling, right? How do you respond? This is a test. You must always remember that all of its whispers are LIES. When it makes you feel that your life is hopeless, you KNOW FOR CERTAIN that thought is a lie. Everything it whispers to you is a lie. So, by definition, you must not believe it when it whispers that your life is hopeless, or that things will never get better. In fact, if it specifically whispers that things will never get better, you should take that as great news. Why? Because everything it says is a lie, so if it says things will not get better, then that means the opposite must be the truth. It means that things WILL get better.

Okay, so what do we have so far? Well, we know depression is a monster that lies, and just tries to whisper things in your head in an effort to convince you that everything is hopeless. We know what it says is a lie. We know to resist and dismiss it. But what about the constant sadness? Even when depression is "silent," it still leaves us in darkness.

The best treatment for darkness is light. I mean that literally. I find the best treatment and coping mechanism for depression is to go outside into the light. The next best thing is exercise. Going for a walk outside is probably the best treatment I can recommend. Obviously, you can go running, hiking, biking, or even just hang out in the park. But you should go out. It is no coincidence that depression feels worse for some people in the evening when it is dark out. So be out in the light as much as possible during the day.

This begs the question, what should you do when it is evening or dark? First, understand that the monster works best when there is a vacuum. There is actually some saying about how the Devil works best in an idle mind, right? A mind that is not occupied is the perfect time for the depression monster to come out and play. Thus, the answer is simple. Do not leave your mind unoccupied during vulnerable times. Do not offer that vacuum for the monster to enter. When you know you might be vulnerable, make sure your mind is fully occupied as much as possible. For example, at night, you might want to have plans for such things as reading, watching TV, listening to music, playing games, or whatever floats your boat. Do NOT just sit around and be sad. If you leave open that vacuum of space, the monster will enter and will start to do what it does until it gets a satisfactory result of triggering you into despair and hopelessness. Do not even give it the chance.

Thus far, we have talked about how to cope with depression so that it no longer controls you. You might be asking, "How do I completely get rid of it?" This is more complicated in the sense that at this point it IS helpful to know what caused it. For example, if you

116

are depressed because someone you love died, then the grieving process becomes a part of actually getting rid of depression. If you are depressed because you had a career setback, or you had a breakup, then you have to address the direct reason by making a plan to move forward from those losses by engaging in new adventures. Ultimately, a person has to let go of what is lost and reach forward into the future for something new. Obviously, you cannot replace or find new people to fix a death you are grieving. But in many cases, and really all cases, some sort of "moving forward" will become necessary.

However, there is another major element in getting completely rid of depression for good. It's called TIME. Getting rid of depression requires time. The more serious the depression, the more time it might take. While some people are depressed for hours, days, or weeks, others are depressed for years. Do not let anyone tell you that your depression has gone on for too long. How do they know how long your depression SHOULD last? Did they experience your loss or trauma? Are they walking in your shoes? Are they God? NO. They do not know, and do not understand. So do not let anyone invalidate your depression, or intensity level of your depression. Yes, it can take years in some cases. But depression will go away. It always goes away or fades over time. Once you stop listening, the monster eventually gives up.

Many people ask whether or not they should take medication for depression. I am not a medical doctor. You should always follow the advice of your trusted medical doctor or mental health professional. But my personal opinion is that medication would certainly be warranted if you are thinking of taking your own life, or if you are unable to function in your daily life at work, school. If medication is what keeps you alive long enough to get a handle on it, then by all means it is a blessing. Many people also need to be able to continue working so that they have money to pay their bills, housing, and food. Medication can be the tape that keeps *you* together in order to keep your life together.

It needs to be noted that medication does not cure depression. Medication treats, or masks, depression so that something even worse does not happen. Therefore, even if you are on medication, you should still follow the suggestions we are discussing, for coping with depression, and ultimately getting rid of depression. Medication is just a tool to help reach our final destination of being free of depression. There is no shame in using that, or any other tools that work.

We discussed recognizing the depression monster for what it is. We discussed calling it out on its bullshit, and those coping mechanisms for dismissing it. We discussed treating darkness with light. Now we need to go back and spend more time discussing how to move forward in your life so that you can move away from depression and leave it.

It is very important you do not go backwards. Do not go back into the darkness of what caused your depression. Always go forwards, and always go toward the light. Always go in the direction of hope, and away from the darkness of the hopelessness of loss or sadness. Identify things that represent light to you. Perhaps it is an activity, a place, certain people, or hopes and dreams. The ideal element is a new adventure filled with what you see as light and hope. You MUST create something for you to look forward to with excitement and hope. Identify what that is for you. Go toward it. Even if you can only take baby steps each day, go ahead and take those steps. As long as you are moving, you will get there. Most importantly, you just want to be moving FORWARD. It is this movement away from the darkness and toward the light that frees you from depression.

I know you can overcome this. I know how much it hurts. I know it makes life seem hopeless. I know how it can go on for what seems like forever. But I promise you things get better. One thing you can depend on in the universe, is that things always change. So, if things are horrible for you right now, you can be guaranteed *that* will change. It is a law of the universe. Things change.

Also, the human spirit has an eternal light and strength that cannot be extinguished. The very fact that you are reading this book is proof that through all of the hopelessness, you still feel deep down inside that things can get better. I can assure you; things WILL get better. You can now see that monster for the lie that it is. You can walk out of the darkness into the light.

While the journey is not always easy or fast, the journey is always very rewarding. You will come out the other side a stronger, wiser, and better person. You will become an example of what makes people great. Fighting through adversity and never giving up is what makes people great. You have the courage to walk through darkness, and the wisdom to walk toward the light. I believe in you, and you should believe in yourself.

You will make it.

You will survive life.

CHAPTER NINETEEN

Structured Task-Driven Lifestyle

The "structured task-driven lifestyle tool" is so incredibly helpful, that I insisted on including it within this book, even though it was exclusive to my book, *Heal Me*. This coping and lifestyle tool was what I used personally during my roughest times. Without it, I would have gotten nothing done during times when I felt I could not do anything at all. I hope you find it was useful as I did, and still do.

The "structured task-driven lifestyle" is an action lifestyle tool used as a coping mechanism to get through daily life. Those who work with me personally know I am always preaching this as the first go-to tool when it comes to pulling us out of a depression or a major setback that has us paralyzed and broken. I wanted to include this concept in the book because some of you might be able to use it in getting productivity back into your life after having suffered a major loss or trauma.

After life deals us a major blow and throws us to the ground, we are often 'down for the count.' When we feel beaten down, defeated, depressed, and hopeless, we often do not have the strength to get back up again. This means we might lay around the house a lot, ignore our tasks and responsibilities, and become very unproductive. If left unchecked, this can lead to problems with work, school, relationships, finances, and home life. When we lose the desire and strength to function properly, we lose our lives, as we know it. What was a personal tragedy or setback, can turn into something that ruins our lives.

You absolutely cannot let that happen. You must take action to save your present lifestyle and future life. I have found the best way to do this is to institute a *structured task-driven lifestyle*. When everything has fallen apart, you have given up, and you cannot function properly, the best thing to do is create a structure that can carry you through, as long as you follow a simple routine.

The structured task-driven lifestyle is based upon a very simple, balanced, daily, and weekly program that is easy to follow, and prompts you to do the productive tasks that must get done, while also including self-care and treats for helping your recovery. The structure is different for everyone. But I will lay out a very common structure so that you get the idea. The premise is that you will set up a schedule and list of tasks a week in advance, and a day in advance.

Let us take a look at a daily schedule first. The ingredients for any given day should include the following:

1. Morning wake-up time and ritual
2. Morning task(s)
3. Exercise
4. Time outside
5. Meals you enjoy
6. Afternoon task(s)
7. Daily treat

8. Personal time
9. Evening ritual and bedtime
10. Sleep

Morning wake-up time and ritual: It is important to have a set time you wake up each morning. It is very critical this first step is done correctly because it sets the tone for the day. If you mess this up, you will likely lose some of the discipline instilled within this lifestyle coping tool. Once you wake up, you need to jump right into your morning rituals. That might include feeding the pets and having your morning coffee. Check your messages and get the house opened up and ready for the day. The point of this step is to start out disciplined, but in a very gentle way. Self-care is important, and two cups of coffee or five minutes to sit staring out the window is totally allowed. This step will also include getting dressed and ready for your day. I mention this step specifically, because changing out of your bed clothes tells your mind and body that it is daytime, and time to get busy. After this step, you are ready for primetime, even if you don't feel ready.

Morning task(s): This is when you look at the task list you completed the night before and jump right into completing those tasks. I often call this the "heavy lifting" of the day. Whatever needs to be done that day which you don't want to do, needs to be done at this time. It is helpful to not give it any thought or hesitation before jumping into this. Just start in. Yeah, you won't feel like it, you won't want to do it, you will think of excuses not to do it, but this is likely one of the most critical steps of the entire day. You must jump in and do these tasks assigned for the day. You will eventually learn that it feels good to do them, and it feels good to do them early, because your day gets easier after this step. This is likely the most unpleasant part of your day. But these things need to get done and doing them will make you feel better.

122

Exercise: I realize this might not be everyone's favorite topic, and that some of you might not include exercise in your lifestyle at all. I am not including exercise in your day because I think you are out of shape or need to lose weight. Nope. I am including it because exercise is one of the best treatments for depression, as well as many other mental challenges. Exercise is a key treatment in your recovery from whatever set you back. I don't care what kind of exercise you do. I am not here to judge you or set an agenda for your fitness. For some of you, exercise might mean walking around your yard for twenty minutes. For others it might mean running several miles. For others it might mean doing twenty sit-ups, and for others it might mean going to the gym. You can spend some time in a pool if you have one handy. You can sit on a stationary bike watching TV. You can do whatever floats your boat. But exercise gets you active so that the mental demons are kept at bay. Exercise kind of re-engages you back into an active life. So, whether it be for only ten minutes or for three hours, please slide it into your daily schedule wherever it is most convenient or works best for you.

Time Outside: Time outside is another of the most effective treatments for depression and anything that ails you. There is something magical about the effects of fresh air and sunlight. If you are clever, you might combine your exercise with your outdoor time. The outdoor time is critical, and even if it means sitting on your front steps for five minutes, please do it. Again, I am not telling you how much or how intense to engage in all of these steps. I am just saying to do all of the steps in some fashion. If you do, you will soon realize the value of doing them.

Meals You Enjoy: Everyone needs to eat. Obviously, it is helpful if you eat healthy. With that said, there is one requirement to this step. It is that you eat something you enjoy. I find it is very helpful if your

123

meals are something you look forward to. So even if you are on a diet or specific meal plan, be sure to include something you enjoy. Mealtime is something to look forward to and enjoy, almost as an incentive.

Afternoon task(s): I find it helpful to break up your daily task list by placing an item or two early in the day, and then another later in the day. The morning ones should be more difficult and unpleasant so that the tasks later in the day are easier. Of course, you may choose to do all of your tasks at once earlier in the day. That's fine. But it is also fine to break it up so that your morning tasks do not seem too overwhelming.

Daily treat. A daily treat is very important. You always need something, or multiple things, to look forward to every day. A treat for yourself is also part of your self-care during recovery. It doesn't matter what it is. You might combine your daily treat with your meals. You might allow yourself a favorite beverage in the evening. You might get an ice cream treat after your exercise. It's up to you. But institute something that you enjoy and that you will look forward to every day.

Personal time: Personal time is free time to do what you want in a leisurely way. This might be spending time online, watching your favorite TV shows, listening to music, reading, or just sitting quietly. It is important for you to have some "down time" every day. I find it most useful when the personal time is done at the end of the day when you are unwinding after your long day. This is your time to slow down and feel good about all you did that day.

Evening ritual and bedtime: This is the opposite of the morning ritual. The first thing you want to do is make sure you complete your task list for the next day. You will need it in the morning. Do not wait to do the task list in the morning. When you wake up, your routine needs to be automatic. Other than doing your task list for the next day, this is a time for shutting down. Do any evening self-care, final TV show, or whatever it is that prepares you for a good night's sleep.

Sleep: Proper sleep is very important. Without proper sleep, you won't be able to do anything on this list correctly, and you will be a mess. Your bedtime should be pretty well set in stone and be sure to give yourself enough hours sleep to feel ready in the morning.

So there you have it. Those are the ingredients for a well-balanced productive day. Yeah, yeah, some of you are ready to criticize the routine I laid out because you have a regular day job, or you have kids to take care of. I fully realize this. I was using this daily routine as an example to show how it works. You have to construct a schedule that works for your specific situation. Everyone's schedule will be a bit different. But it is important you include all of the items on the list.

That brings us to the next part of the discussion. How you order and implement all of the ingredients is what I call "the arc of the day." The arc of the day is an attempt to create a natural arc with all of the ingredients so that your day flows smoothly, productively, with the least amount of misery, and with the most amount of joy.

Imagine an arc, like a rainbow. At the bottom is the morning when you wake up. The arc starts at the ground. You are just starting out. Then you start to climb up the arc. This is when you are doing your heavy lifting of morning tasks for the day. Not easy. But then you get past that and reach the peak, or top of the arc. This is where you might be doing your outside time, exercise, or lunch.

You are well into your day and your heavy lifting climb up the arc is behind you. Now you will begin descending down the other side of the arc. This is when you might be doing an easier task, having some personal time, or enjoying dinner. Finally, the downside of the arc touches the ground again and you are going to bed.

The idea of "the arc of the day" is to make sure the arc is working well for you. Do not put something difficult and miserable on the downside of the arc. Don't try to do something difficult right when the arc is about to touch ground again for the night. Make sure you are doing something satisfying at the top of the arc. Now you see why I inserted the more difficult unpleasant tasks at the beginning of the day when you are climbing up the arc. All of your ingredients should fit naturally into the daily arc, if possible.

If you have a regular day-job and cannot do this, then what you can do is create mini arcs. For example, you will have one mini arc in the morning, then your regular workday, then another mini arc after work. So if you get out of work toward the end of the day, you would be starting up the front side of the mini arc. So do your most difficult task right after work. Then perhaps your exercise or whatever at the peak of your arc, then make your way down the easier backside of the arc as you aim toward bedtime. The arc of the day idea still works. You just might have to have smaller arcs, or a couple of different arcs each day.

Everything I described above is how to create a daily arc. You also need to construct a weekly arc. The concept is exactly the same for the weekly arc as it was for the daily arc. We will say that Monday morning is the bottom of the front side of the arc, and Sunday night is the bottom of the backside of the weekly arc. So how would you build this arc? Well, Monday and Tuesday we are climbing up the front side of the arc. Monday and Tuesday might be the days we put our least pleasant tasks. Wednesday and Thursday are the days where we are reaching the peak of the arc. Hopefully by then you have completed your worst tasks of the week. Perhaps Wednesday and Thursday are good days for going out and doing something social, or some weekly activity you enjoy. Then Friday, Saturday, and Sunday you are climbing down the backside of the arc. Ideally, you would put in your easiest and most enjoyable tasks and activities here. Be sure later on Sunday you start to wind down the week so you can prepare for another week. Sunday would be the day to do a task list for the upcoming week. Hopefully you get the idea.

Again, if you have a work schedule or something that messes with this structure, you can still use the arc of the week idea by instituting multiple arcs. For example, if you do all of your weekly tasks on the weekend, you would have a mini arc that just covers Saturday and Sunday. So, use that as your arc. You might guess by now that I would suggest doing your most difficult tasks Saturday morning, and then being more leisurely Sunday afternoon.

Yes, people also do monthly arcs. Some people have a monthly task list and tackle everything difficult the first part of the month, and then do something special toward the end of the month. The possibilities are endless. If you find yourself wanting to do a yearly arc or ten-year arc, then we might have to discuss a potential compulsive disorder, haha. But I'm all for it if you can sell its benefits and make it help you in great ways.

I am truly hoping that you see the benefit of using such a structured approach to help your recovery from depression and traumas. If we do not have any approach at all, it is possible that we end up motionless for weeks and months, or even years. People can lose everything if they do not pick themselves back up again.

My structured task-driven lifestyle and arc of the day approach is a way for people to construct something they can blindly follow that will put them onto a path to recovery much faster. In addition, you will be functioning properly and taking care of your responsibilities so that you do not make your situation worse than it already is. With this tool, you will be back up and running, and perhaps end up more productive than you ever were before. I hope it can help you in some way. All of the skills and tools you can possibly learn will help you survive life.

CHAPTER TWENTY

Sun Shine So Bright

The sun shines so bright

But my heart still feels dark like night

I remain inside while looking out

I can see the sun is out while I pout

Why do I feel so cloudy even in sunlight?

My insides feel like the rain at night

I can't change the sun and I can't change the night

But I can decide to feel more bright

The clouds may remain, and the rain may continue to fall
But I choose to look outside at the sun instead of bawl

Instead of staying inside and just staring out
It's much better to walk outside in the sun without a doubt

Now that I am outside hoping for healing to begin
I start to feel the warmth of the sun from deep within

My apologies, as I am not a poet, and I certainly know it.

Brian Hunter 2022

CHAPTER TWENTY-ONE

Who Are You?

I am not asking you who you are. I am asking you to ask yourself if you know who you are. People who fully understand who they are have a much easier time surviving life.

Sometimes it is easier to start with understanding who we are not. You were raised a certain way by your parents, in a certain culture. Is that who you are? Are you who your parents raised you to be? Or, are you the result of how you were raised in a toxic environment? These questions can be mutually exclusive, related, or both true at the same time.

Different people will have very different reactions to these questions. There are plenty of people who had wonderful parents, and those parents did a wonderful job raising them. You might credit your parents for making you into the wonderful person that you feel you are today. Perhaps YOU ARE indeed the person your parents raised you to be. There is nothing wrong with that.

For others, it is a totally different story. Others may have been subjected to various levels of toxicity during their childhood. Their parents may have tried to raise them in certain ways, and those ways may have been toxic, or at least not in line with the person's true self.

This is especially true if you grew up in an abusive environment as a child. This environment during your childhood might have turned you into a person who is traumatized, timid, skittish, highly aggressive, and defensive. In other words, you might be the person that you are from your upbringing, and not necessarily who you feel you truly are, or who your soul thinks you are, not to mention who you WANT to be.

Which is it for you? Are you truly who you are, and are happy about it? Or are you someone who is not who they are supposed to be because of a toxic environment?

It is not just a toxic environment during childhood that can turn you into someone you are not. Society can do it also. School can do it. Friends can do it. Romantic relationships can do it.

An example of this might be the person who was a great student in high school, and always got great grades. If this was you, teachers and everyone else may have labeled you as someone who would go onto college and become a lawyer or doctor, or something like that. That is who they tried to make you. That is who they thought you were. But maybe that is not the person you felt you were inside. Despite getting great grades in school, maybe you had no interest in college. Maybe you had other passions to chase. Maybe you were more social, and had little interest in academics, even though you did well in them. Maybe you wanted to be an artist. Maybe you were a free spirit and wanted to travel.

In the above example, the person who doesn't know who they are, might have continued on to college to become a lawyer or something like that, even though that was not their inner truth. This person might not fully know who they are. They might just be going with the identity that everyone else had assigned them. This person would likely end up becoming very unhappy since they would be pursuing a life that is not in alignment with their true self.

It is important to fully understand who you truly are, and not let

132

others define it for you. If you let others define your own self identify for you, it will mean that you will end up feeling lost, misplaced, and very unhappy.

This problem of identity can become a huge issue in relationships. Your partner might think of you in a certain way that does not match how you think of yourself. Worse yet, your partner might try to force you to be the person THEY want you to be, rather than allowing you to be who you truly are.

This type of thing becomes toxic in a relationship, and I guarantee that your relationship will either not work, or you will end up being very unhappy in the relationship. It is important that you and your partner reconcile this issue and fix it. Either they need to accept you for who you truly feel you are, or you both need to consider going your separate ways.

But before you even get to that point, you have to first be certain that YOU know who you are. Up to this point, we have been discussing who you are not. But after you recognize those points, you need to then focus on who you ARE.

Do you know who you are? Sometimes it can be helpful to write down on a piece of paper who you think you are. How would you define yourself? What kind of person are you? What are your likes and dislikes? What are your dreams? What are your goals in life? How do you often feel? How do you wish you would feel? What kind of people do you enjoy being with? What are your passions? You can come up with your own questions as well. The idea is for you to truly define who you are.

What can be a fun exercise is for you to write down a bunch of questions like this. Then, go ahead and fill out your answers. If you have a partner, have them also answer the questions, but from their perspective. It can be funny to see how similarly, or differently, your partner answers the questions about who you are. Is your partner able to answer the questions fairly accurately about who you are? Or does your partner seem to have a totally different perspective of who you are? The answer to that can be funny and enlightening (and scary).

What can also be enlightening, is to see how you might struggle at answering some of the questions about yourself. Maybe you will even struggle to answer some of the questions at all. How is it possible that you cannot easily answer all of the questions? You would be surprised how many people struggle with this exercise. This would be proof that you do not know who you are.

Setting aside how your partner did, or would do, on the questions about defining who you are, let us focus on you and your perspectives on yourself. If you know who you are, then your work here is done. But if you feel you have some work left to do, let us continue.

The first step in confirming your true identity, is to be sure to deconstruct all of the old labels that your parents, family, friends, and society, have projected onto you that are not part of your true self. After you write down your own definition of who you think you are, you should be able to compare that with how those around you see you.

Once you can identify the labels that are not part of your true self, you can begin to mentally detach those from your identity, and from your very being. It is okay to gently and politely begin refusing to own those old labels that are not part of your true identity. You can say things to others like, "I know everyone thinks I am that way, but in reality, that is not really me." After you say things like that many times, over a period of time, those around you will start to get the message that you are working on redefining yourself. Hopefully they will respect and abide by what you are doing. If they do not, it still should not stop you from continuing with the process.

After you have worked through a process of deconstructing the labels and identities that others have put upon you, it is time to begin asserting and strengthening the identity of how you see your true self. Be sure to constantly evaluate and re-evaluate who you think you are. It is okay to keep asking yourself the question of who you are. It is healthy to keep writing down your current definitions of who you think you are. See if it has changed at all, or if it seems to be remaining consistent.

As long as you can see that your own vision of your identity is remaining fairly constant, you should continue to reinforce those labels and identities upon yourself. You may also do this in a very obvious and social way so that everyone around you can also benefit from seeing the confirmations and validations of who you truly are.

This process I have outlined is not something that simply starts and ends. It is a process that is forever in the making. It is a work in progress. It can also change as you change. It is okay to change who you are. The important thing is that you are in total control of who you are, and that you control the changes to who you are becoming.

You must be the master of your domain. You must have a strong sense of 'self,' and a strong knowing of who you are. You must be able to clearly answer the question of who you are. Life can be a huge struggle, and it is only more difficult if you are not sure of who you truly are.

Figuring out who you truly are as a person, and as a soul, can be a very freeing experience. You will find that you feel much better, and healthier, once you are living more in alignment of your true identity. You will also be less likely to be manipulated by those who think they can control your identity. Don't give up ownership of your identity to anyone, including society, and those closest to you.

Always own your identity. It is yours. It is your gift of freedom from God and the universe. You are free to be you, and you are free to be who you want to be.

If you do not like who you are, then change who you are. You have the freedom to do this as well. This kind of self-work is not always easy, but it is very liberating. I want you to be free. When you are free, you can be happy. This is my wish for you.

CHAPTER TWENTY-TWO

Who Should You Listen To?

When you are lost and confused, or even just young and inexperienced, you might wonder who you should be listening to. You will have all kinds of people yelling advice, commands, and rants at you. These people might include parents, siblings, extended family, teachers, mentors, bosses, co-workers, and strangers on the street. Some of these people may be very smart and experienced. Should you listen to them when trying to make choices about your life? Also, what happens when the advice and "words of wisdom" from these folks contradict one another? Who do you believe?

The correct proper answer to the above questions is to listen to all of them. The correct real answer is to not listen to any of them in terms of blindly doing what they tell you to do. Let me explain. You should LISTEN to everyone. Usually everyone has at least one small morsel of useful information or experience to impart. But just because you are listening to them does not mean you have to act upon their advice.

Have I cleared all of this up for you yet? Are we done with this subject and ready to move on? Glad I could help clarify things for you. Yes, you're welcome, anytime.

OH? Or maybe not? Okay. Then let me try to clarify some things. When everyone is spouting conflicting advice at you, you should listen to all of it. But you shouldn't act upon any of it without further consideration.

Why didn't I just say it like that in the first place? I can be so annoying sometimes. But here is the important part. How do you decide WHO to listen to more carefully, and trust to guide your final direction? I have an answer for that, and I know how you can find that person. Go look in the mirror. You will see the person who you need to listen to the most.

Let's say that you are lost and confused, much like me writing this chapter. You have some life choices to make, and you don't know what to do. Worse yet, you don't know where to turn for advice. If you ask those around you, they are all giving you different answers. Some of the answers are from smart people, and the answers do seem smart. But you don't know if their advice is a true fit for you and your situation. So even though you have heard all kinds of advice, you still don't know what to do.

Go to the one person who might know. Look in the mirror. Say, "I need some answers." If you start answering back and having a long conversation, then it means you are like me and have probably spent too much time alone writing books. But let me help you with this.

First, think about your own situation and your question. Make sure you clearly understand your predicament, and the precise question you are hoping to find answers for. Then ask yourself, "How do I want to feel?"

You might reply to yourself with a variety of answers. I cannot, and should not, tell you what your reply is. You need to decide for yourself what your reply is. But some examples might be, "I want to feel inspired." "I want to feel excited." "I want to feel safe and secure." "I want to feel free." "I want to feel happy." "I want to feel calm and at peace." "I want to feel loved." You get the idea. But you need to seriously consider your answer carefully and come up with how you truly want to feel in regard to your current question.

Once you have settled on your final answer, you have a beacon of light to aim for, and move toward. You have set yourself a goal. Achievable or not, a goal is important. The advice you take, and act upon, should be in alignment with you arriving at your final destination of "how you want to feel."

After this step is complete, you can start to truly listen to what others have to say. People who are smart and more experienced than you probably know the best ways of reaching your chosen destination. But always evaluate their advice in terms of how successfully it will get you to your destination. Sometimes people's advice is very good and very effective, but it will cause you to arrive at the wrong destination.

Once you choose what seems to be the best and most relevant advice for your situation, act upon it. Do not be afraid to consult with the person who gave you the advice. In a way, this makes the person who gave you the advice more accountable, and they may end up helping you further since it was their advice that you acted upon.

Additionally, do not be afraid to change course, or make adjustments if things are not working as you had hoped. Sometimes even good advice won't work with certain people, in certain situations, at certain times. If something is not working, and it seems like it is not going to work, make a change. Try some similar advice that is relevant to your final destination or try a different approach to the same advice.

Let's recap. You are lost and confused, and you don't know what to do. Everyone gives you different advice and insists that their advice is the correct advice. You listen, but don't act upon it yet. Instead, you have some quiet moments of meditation and contemplation amongst yourself. You think about your situation, and your question. You ask yourself, "How do I want to feel?" You come up with your answer. Notice that this first process is all internal within yourself for the most part. YOU are the person who needs to be consulted. Only YOU can decide how you want to feel. Therefore, you are the only person who can decide what the final destination should be. But once you have set your final destination, the next process is mostly external. You are going to purposely and aggressively, reach out to others for the best possible advice. Listen to the smartest and most experienced people you know. They will have the best ideas on how to reach your final destination.

Now you can see why my initial answers about who to listen to were so confusing. It truly is nobody, and everybody, but mostly yourself. Sort of. Except now my riddles and confusion do not seem so unclear and stupid. I think you got this now.

But one last thing. It is okay to re-evaluate your initial question to yourself. Things change, life changes, and you change. So, every once in a while, ask yourself, "How do I want to feel?" See if your answer is the same, or if it has changed at all. If your answer has changed, then consider adjusting your final destination. If you do that, then make sure to get fresh advice on the best ways to get there. You don't need to be lost and confused. As long as you can figure out "how you want to feel," you can figure out which way to go, and you can listen to everyone who might be able to help you get there. But whatever you do, only listen to yourself when it comes to what you truly want, and how you truly want to feel. You will have a much easier time surviving life if you stick to your own truth. Your soul will lead the way.

CHAPTER TWENTY-THREE

What To Do When Nothing Else Works

Sometimes we feel at the end of our rope and don't even have the energy to get up. We feel the walls closing in around us, and feel that we are completely isolated, trapped, and do not see much hope. If you feel that your normal coping mechanisms are not working, or you feel particularly depleted and broken, then consider some of the ideas and thoughts below:

ALL THINGS ARE TEMPORARY. Remember that your mind and mood will play tricks on you and will try to fool you into thinking that everything is hopeless, and nothing will ever get better. The monster in your mind, the monster of depression, can be very convincing. There can be moments when you are CERTAIN that things are hopeless and will never get better. REMEMBER THAT THIS IS A LIE! Nothing is permanent, nothing is hopeless, and eventually things get better. Do NOT let the monster in your mind fool you and convince you otherwise.

141

GO OUTSIDE. Even if you don't feel like it, go outside. The best-case scenario is that you go for a walk or a hike someplace you enjoy. If you cannot do that, then just go outside and walk around a little bit. Or maybe just stand outside. Even if you are tired and moving at the speed of a sloth, you still need to go outside. If it's nice outside, stay out there for a bit and let the sun shine on you. If it's not nice outside, just get some moments of fresh air. Being outside can work miracles in a very short period of time.

REMEMBER THAT YOU ARE OF GREAT VALUE, EVEN IF NOBODY SEES IT OR ACKNOWLEDGES IT. There might be times when you feel unwanted or invisible. The monster in your mind will try to trick you into thinking that NOBODY wants you, and that everyone hates you. IT'S A LIE! When you are feeling very down, you might believe the lie, because it seems so convincing and clear in that moment. You have to remember that what you are seeing in that moment is just a tiny slice of your reality in one of your worst moments. It is not the real or complete truth. Do not let the negative situation and monster in your mind fool you into thinking you have no value. Maybe you need to poke around in this book again.

LISTEN TO MUSIC OR WATCH A FAVORITE TV SHOW/MOVIE. You need to be pulled out of your horrible moment somehow. Listening to music or watching a TV show or movie can pull you out of your current negative reality. I should also add reading to this. I will be honest and give a pathetic shameless plug at the same time, by saying that when I am feeling down, I dip into my Living A Meaningful Life book series. I don't do this because I am a narcissist enjoying my own books. I do this because what I wrote in that series was literally my 'happy place,' a depiction of how people should be acting and treating each other. So, I sometimes need that medicine for my soul. Look at the books you enjoy, or your favorite music or TV shows. Even getting a half an hour of relief from your current hard time can be enough to give you the perspective you need to deal with your feelings and situation more logically and effectively. Do not be afraid to use all coping mechanisms available to you. You are fighting your own negative psychology, and all tools should be made available to help you in your fight.

MESSAGE OR CALL A FRIEND. Sometimes this is the first option. But not all of us have friends or family we can talk to, and our support system of people might not always be available. But certainly, talking with your support system is one of the best things you can possibly do.

REACH OUT TO OTHERS. This suggestion might be confusing at first. Didn't I already suggest reaching out to your support system of family and friends? Yes, I did. But what I mean by this particular suggestion of "reaching out to others," is reaching out for any human interaction. Even if it is saying "Hi" to a stranger. Even the most simple and limited human interaction can be helpful in our dark times. Another facet of this suggestion is for you to reach out to others who might need YOUR help. This might seem odd for me to suggest that you help others when you yourself need help the most, but helping others is medicine for your soul. Doing small random acts of kindness will make you feel better, and also provide human interaction. Do for others what you wish people would do for you. This expression of "need" and "giving" combine together to provide love for your own soul through your own actions toward others. I got through some of my worst times by helping others. They may not have realized how much pain I was in at the time, but I felt better after knowing that I was helpful to others who really needed me.

The biggest thing for me to stress again, is to remind you that EVERYTHING changes eventually, and FOR CERTAIN, your current situation IS going to change. You just need to give it a chance to do so.

When you feel at a complete loss, and you are just "so done," your strategy needs to be self-care. Your focus needs to be giving yourself what you need in order to survive a little longer, until you can feel a little better. Use all of your go-to coping mechanisms to keep yourself calm while you wait for time to pass. Trust me, you will feel better, given enough time. These waves of extreme hopelessness and depletion come and go. You just need to keep yourself together while you wait for it to fade out again.

Surviving life is not easy. Everyone has their rough times. If you ask a 90-year-old if they had rough times, they would tell you that they had multiple periods of rough times. But they would also say that those rough times eventually passed. It is very hard for younger people to realize this. They have not had the benefit of seeing the big picture over a long period of time yet. But the reality is that over a long life, you will have some bad periods. During those bad periods, you will feel that it is hopeless and will never get better. But it will. The 90-year-old would tell you this.

You have to hang in there through the rough times in order to enjoy the fun, satisfaction, and even euphoria, of the good times. Life is an adventure, and not an easy one. Some people have it easier than others. Some of you probably think I am being overly dramatic, or even negative. Others of you might think I am not being dramatic enough, and not adequately describing the deep pain involved. I understand both sides.

But this chapter is for those suffering the most in this moment. While I might not know you, and your struggle is unique to you, I do understand how painful things can be. I've been there, in my own unique struggles. But right now, you are the one who matters most, and I want you to be okay. Please give yourself a chance. I know you can survive life. There are incredible wonders out there for you to discover and experience. You have no idea what is in store for your future. Wait until you see the surprises waiting and wait until you see the positive rewards waiting for you down the road. Hang in there. Much love to you.

CHAPTER TWENTY-FOUR

If I Sat Here Near Death

If I sat here near death, and I could impart to you any information, blessing, or answers, what would it be? For anyone sitting near death, physically, mentally, emotionally, in reality, or figuratively, it means seeing things differently than everyone else. The view is broad and philosophical. It is not about sweating the small stuff.

If you could ask me one last question before my death, what would it be? Maybe nothing? Or maybe you would have some kind of weird philosophical question? Maybe you are just creeped out by the entire question and proposition. Why would that be?

Are you not comfortable thinking of death? Is it scary to you? When you think of someone else dying, is your first thought the fear of losing them, or is it the reminder that eventually you will get your turn?

My goal with this chapter is not to scare and traumatize everyone. Believe me, I could go very in-depth into all of this, and more or less write an entire book just on this subject. I have given the subject of death endless thought. I have imagined myself dead, and I have come up with my own theories of what happens after we die. This book, and even this chapter, is not about that, though. This entire book is about LIFE. However, if you have an interest in taking a peek at what my theories on death are, you can find all of that in my book, *The Hunter Equation*.

I am not afraid of death. Nor should you be. For this reason, I am comfortable discussing it. It is helpful to discuss aging and death as a way of providing perspective into how we are LIVING our lives.

If I were sitting here near death, and you were curious to hear my parting thoughts, I would have a few thoughts to share. I would tell you that the only things that matter are meaningful things. The pointless details of society do not matter. What matters are your relationships, and the things you did to make a difference for other people, your community, and the world. People might remember what you did for work, and what you had, but the only thing that will affect them emotionally are the things you did to change their lives.

People will remember any kindness, compassion, and love you extended to them. People will remember patience and grace given by you. They will remember how you treated them and others. They will remember if you made them laugh, cry, or think. These are all meaningful things.

I would also remind you that experiences are why we are here. We are here to experience places, people, emotions, and sensations. So, travel much, interact with a broad range of people, dare to feel a broad range of emotions, and indulge in all of the human sensations available to you.

I would remind you that you have the freedom to choose how you live your life, and what kind of person you want to be. I would warn you that struggle, and pain are a part of life. But I would encourage you to overcome the temptation to give up too soon on your dreams.

Your dreams are yours to choose and are a gift from God and the universe. Others will criticize your dreams and try to get you to give them up. They do this because they already gave up their dreams, and they want company in their misery for doing so.

I would ask you to not fixate on my mistakes and my shortcomings, but rather focus on my courage, strength, and willingness to always do the right things as best I could. I would like to say this about you as well. I would say that there is no such thing as a bad person because they failed, as long as they always strived to do what was right. I would remind you to not be like me or others. I would encourage you to be yourself, whoever and whatever that means to you.

I would hope that my death would serve as a reminder that life is limited. You only have so much time here on Earth. How will you use it? Will you waste time? How much time will you waste before you realize that wasting time is a waste of time?

I would urge you to discover everything. Discover yourself. Discover people, especially those who touch your soul. Discover the Earth you live on. Discover all you can. Life is about discovery and experiences you have along the way.

Don't be afraid. Fear only serves to limit you. Fear is a chain that serves to paralyze and trap you. Do not be afraid of failure, and do not let failure cause you to fail. There is no failure for those who had the courage to try, and are willing to try again, or try other things. Failure is only a label used by those who are afraid to try.

If you suffer mistakes and setbacks in life, try to move on from them as quickly as possible. Sitting in them serves no purpose other than to waste your time here and make your situation even worse. Get back up in all of your tears and start walking forward again.

I hope you see and hear my message loud and clear. My advice to you would be to live your life, live it fully, and live it with meaning.

If you asked me how I would want to be remembered, I would say to you, "Remember me in a way that inspires you to live your life with as much meaning as possible."

But I am not done yet, and neither is this chapter. There is another purpose to examining this notion of being near death. This is a reality check for you. Imagine yourself speaking with me as I am near my death. Think about how that might affect how you think of your own life, and how you are currently living your own life.

Based upon the reflections I have offered, does this change how you want to live your life? Are there changes you want to make? What are they? Perhaps you want to live your life more in alignment with the broader and more meaningful perspective of life which I have offered?

I have an even more precise question to ask. Consider for a moment if you were in my hypothetical position of sitting near death. Would you have regrets about how you lived your life? Would you have regrets of how you are presently living your life?

My suggestion to you would be to make some changes so that you are currently living your life more in alignment with how you would wish you had lived your life, if you were near the end.

When you are near the end, you won't remember many of the fine details and chores of your life. But you will remember how you lived, how you treated others, your relationships, and the impact you made upon your circle of people, your community, and the world. The broader things start to matter more. So, pay attention to the broader things more. Live in a way that would make you comfortable in the event that life was ending.

Life is precious. Do you know why? Life is precious because it ends. It is limited. Anything that is limited and ends, is precious. Like everything that is precious and limited, live life wisely and fully before it is gone.

Never forget that love wins over hate, and compassion wins over greed. Freedom is your gift to decipher and discern what is right and wrong. Treat others in a way that will make them remember you positively when you are gone.

Love be with you always.

CHAPTER TWENTY-FIVE

Your Spirit Must Endure

Your spirit must endure. We need you. I am speaking to all of you, but for different reasons. If you are feeling great, and your spirit is strong and vibrant, WE NEED YOU. We need your enthusiasm, love, and inspiration. Please. Your positive energy is food for the starving souls. Be kind and be generous. Offer your love and encouragement to those who need it. You are the rocket fuel that propels us to new heights.

Conversely, if you are someone who is in pain and struggling, and your spirit feels wounded, and cries for love and help, WE NEED YOU. The fact you are in pain and that your spirit cries, is proof that you carry an abundance of empathy within your soul.

There are great and wonderful people with a very diverse set of circumstances, both good and bad. Those who are truly blessed will understand our need to focus on those who are struggling and in pain right now. So forgive me for doing so. Those who are feeling strong and able, should extend their hand to those who need a hand.

I know some of you are hurting deeply or have been hurt in the past. Your spirit feels damaged, or worse. Maybe you feel broken. Some of us have experienced the "walking dead" sensation, when our spirit feels vacant or missing. This often results from an overload of trauma, along with a lack of hope.

But your spirit is still there. It's like a candle that sits idle, and just needs to be reignited. We need to reignite your candle. But I have to explain why this is so important to do.

It really does come down to empathy. Empathy is the basis upon which humanity thrives or dies. Without empathy, humanity will be sick and gradually decay. It will feed upon its own dying flesh until it is extinguished to nothing. But with empathy, humanity only becomes stronger and more vibrant. Empathy is based in love, and love lives with empathy. Empathy is the light that shines. It gives us hope and it shows us the way. Its warmth gives us comfort in cold and dark times. It reminds us that we are never alone in the dark.

Here lies the irony. Often those in the darkest places are the ones with the most light of empathy. Having empathy means that you feel pain very easily, and at higher levels. Not only do you feel your own pain more deeply, but you feel the pain of others, and even the world in general.

When someone hurts you, it reverberates throughout your entire body, mind, and soul. You take it more personally. You don't understand cruelty. To you, cruelty is a foreign concept, and how it can even exist is a mystery to you.

A person who operates on a basis of love and empathy, often assumes that others do and should as well. But they do not. There are a lot of people void of empathy out there, and others who have shut it off for one reason or another. Sometimes abused or damaged people end up shutting off their empathy as a survival coping mechanism.

This is why when I see a person with no empathy, I try not to rush to judgement. I ask myself if this is a person who has been a victim of cruelty and shut off their empathy out of self-preservation, or is this a person who is not capable of empathy, and is quite dangerous? People without empathy are very dangerous because they have no inhibitions or circuit breakers in how they are willing to behave, or what they are willing to do to others. We call them sociopaths, psychopaths, or worse.

But I am not focusing on them. I am focusing on those who are the opposite. I am focusing on those with an abundance of empathy, who are in pain because of it. You deserve our love, understanding, and yes, our empathy.

Your spirit is empathy, and empathy comprises your spirit. Humanity needs empathy. We all need empathy. Therefore, we need your spirit, and we need you. We need you and your spirit to endure.

So, if you are someone who is feeling pain very deeply because of your abundance of empathy, you need to realize some things. First, you are not alone, and there IS a logical explanation for why you seem to experience pain at deeper levels than most.

Your empathy causes you to be extra-sensitive to all emotional sensations. If someone hurts you, it will hurt you deeply. If you are feeling alone, you will feel lonely at deeper levels than others. If you have been abandoned, you will have trouble comprehending how the abandonment against you was even possible. If you have been a victim of cruelty, you will remain stunned and confused as to what even happened, and how anyone could have ever done that to you. When someone betrays you, it comes as a complete surprise, because your own empathy would have never allowed you to do that to someone else. Yet, it was done to you, so you are left dazed and confused, as well as broken.

Our empathy can leave us a bit vulnerable, and even naïve. We are sitting targets for those with less empathy, or worse yet, sociopaths. But this leads me back to my original point. The decay or survival of humanity depends upon empathy.

So, if you have an abundance of empathy, then the survival of humanity depends on you. Am I being overly dramatic? It sounds that way. But I'm not. I am being practical and logical.

Once enough of humanity is lacking in empathy, it will be over. Therefore, it is absolutely critical that those with empathy remain strong and present. You must hold the line. You are the inspiration of how we should be, what we should be, and you possess what will decide the fate of humanity.

Thus, we need you. Quite literally. It wasn't just a clever phrase. It was a literal statement of need. We need as much empathy in this world as we can muster.

If you experience great pain, and a deep pain, because you are a person who has great amounts of empathy, then you are very much needed, valued, and loved. Please remember this. Think of this often. I know this might not be much consolation for your pain and suffering, but you need to know that the kind of person you are, and your qualities, are appreciated and needed. Your suffering is not in vain. You play a valuable role as part of humanity itself. You are the future. Your ability to maintain your empathy determines our future.

Your empathy is your spirit. Your spirit lights the world. Your spirit will save us all. Therefore, your spirit must endure. Never forget this. When you are in pain, or feel wronged by others, remember what I have said here. Hold onto it tightly, as if it is a hug given to you. Take comfort within your own light. Your call to hold the light is a necessary one, and a valiant one. Be proud and stand tall. Don't let them get you down. Stand strong within the storm whipping around you. Trust in your eternal light and know that YOU hold the light. It can only be extinguished if you turn away and give up. As long as you still believe in your own light, it will never go out. It will keep you warm, and it will light your way. You will never be alone, for you remain close to the light of God and the universe. Bless you, and your light of empathy. May your spirit always endure.

CHAPTER TWENTY-SIX

Hope

What is hope? Hope is life. Without hope, there is no life. In my opinion, hope is more important than water or food. Plenty of people have died from having no hope even though they had plenty of food and water. Plus, you can go without food and water for a certain period of time as long as you have hope that relief is coming. So, there you have it.

Hope is the key to life, and without it we can't survive life. Perhaps this should have been the first chapter, if it is so important? No. It is the last chapter because it is the most important. If you forget everything else, do not forget about hope. Let this chapter be the one that sits with you after you get up from reading this book and walk away.

Hope is easy to lose. There is the monster in our head always busy trying to hide hope, or completely kill it. The monster wants to trick us into thinking that hope is gone, and that there is no hope ever coming back. These are always lies. There is always hope. Where there is life, there is hope; and where there is hope, there is life.

Hope is everything. It sustains our spirit, and it sustains our life.

Hope inspires us and excites us. Many of us live only because of hope. You must always reserve a safe place in your soul for hope.

The secret to surviving life is keeping hope alive. I believe strongly that each person must create a lifestyle that fosters hope.

Too many people view hope as an external force which they hope will smile upon them and visit them often. This is not smart. This provides distance between you and hope, and it takes any control of holding hope out of your hands and leaves it up to chance.

It is much smarter for you to grab hope, hold it, embrace it, and make it a permanent part of your life. This way, it is less likely that hope can be stolen from you. Make hope a part of you. Keep it in your heart and in your soul. Always keep it in your mind so that you never forget it is there.

The way to do this is by making hope a part of your daily lifestyle. When you wake up in the morning, think of what you are hopeful for in that day, and what specific things make you hopeful. Make sure you engage in activities each day that seem to always give you hope. You can call this "self-care."

Getting outside, going for walks, and thinking about what you hope to do, or things that you are working toward because you hope to achieve certain things, is a great way to keep hope alive in your daily life. Walk with hope hand in hand wherever you go. Never let hope go.

Hope is eternal. Even when we leave this Earth, there is still hope. We have hope for our souls, and we have hope for those we eventually leave behind. We have hope for what the world and humanity can become. We have so much love and hope for our loved ones. We should die with hope when our time eventually comes. When I said life is hope and hope is life, I was only stating part of the whole truth. Hope is not just life. Hope is even more than that. Hope is everything.

My hope for you is that you will never lose hope. I have tried to give you enough in this book so that you can always find hope no matter what you are facing in life. I am certain that you can survive life. I have tried to provide some tools to help you, but your biggest asset, your biggest hope, is yourself.

Your soul, your spirit, your strength, your courage, your ability to face all of your traumas in life, they all give me inspiration. I try to pay this back by turning my inspiration into love and advice to you. I hope you have enjoyed this as much as I have. I hope you accomplish amazing things in your life. I hope you achieve all of your dreams. I know that you can. Anything is possible. BELIEVE.

Bless you, and much love to you in your journey of life.

If you enjoyed this book and are not ready for the journey to be over, may I suggest the following books which will allow you to continue on your journey, with me still cheering you along.

Heal Me is my book providing helpful thoughts and advice about recovering from a wide range of life traumas.

Rising To Greatness is my book providing a more structured process of restarting or rebooting your life.

EVOLVE is my more advanced and futuristic approach to self-improvement and raising yourself up to the next level of humanity.

My 'Living A Meaningful Life' book series is my 'happy place,' and I think it could be yours, too. It is a family saga about what can be right in this world, and how we can live our lives more in alignment with values that allow us to live more meaningful lives.

Acknowledgments

Thank you Sarah Delamere Hurding, for your editorial assistance, encouragement, and endless support.

Thanks to all of my clients and benefactors who have supported my mission of helping people become greater, stronger, more self-empowered, enlightened, and free of pain.

ABOUT THE AUTHOR

Brian Hunter is an American Author and Life Coach based in Los Angeles, California. However, Brian started life with a rural upbringing, surrounded by small towns, farms, lakes, and the peace of nature. Brian is the author of the epic book series, 'Living A Meaningful Life,' as well as numerous self-help and genre books, including, *Surviving Life, EVOLVE, Heal Me, Rising To Greatness, The Hunter Equation, Aliens,* and *The Walk-In.* His books have sold around the world and have been Best Sellers within their genres. Brian was acknowledged as being intuitive as a child, and then later in life was attributed as having psychic abilities. Brian has worked with people from all over the world, including celebrities and captains of industry. Brian was an original cast member of the TV series pilot Missing Peace, in which psychics worked with detectives to solve cold cases. He has also worked as an actor and model in Hollywood and been featured in various movie and TV productions. Brian's current focus is on his writing and life coaching work, helping clients from all walks of life.

www.brianhunterhelps.com

ALSO, BY BRIAN HUNTER

Heal Me is a powerful and touching book that will pull at your heartstrings, give you practical advice on overcoming a variety of life traumas, and will put you on the road to recovery and healing. *Heal Me* examines such issues as the death of a loved one, loss of a pet, suicide, anxiety, addiction, life failures, major life mistakes, broken relationships, abuse, sexual assault, self-esteem, living in a toxic world surrounded by toxic people, loneliness, and many other issues. This is a self-care book written in a very loving, practical, and informative way that you can gift to yourself, family, young people, and friends, as a gesture of love, support, and hope.

Rising To Greatness is the companion book to Heal Me and is a self-help book that takes you on a step-by-step transformation, from the ashes of being broken and lost, to the greatness of self-empowerment, accomplishment, and happiness. This book includes such topics as developing your sense of self, eliminating fear from your life, mastering your emotions, self-discipline and motivation, communication skills, and so much more.

EVOLVE is a cutting-edge, unique, powerful, and practical personal transformation self-help improvement book, which examines human life and all of its issues from a unique futuristic approach with a touch of humor. A selection of topics include healing from personal losses and traumas, coping with sadness and depression, moving past fear that others use to control, manipulate, and abuse you, clarity in thinking, advanced communication skills, evolving your relationships, exploring the meaning of life, how everything in the Universe is connected, developing your psychic ability, and a little discussion about aliens possibly living among us. Yes, there is everything, which is all directly tied back to your own personal life.

Living A Meaningful Life is an epic book series, with numerous installments, that will change your life. We are all capable of doing extraordinary things. We must only decide within ourselves to BE extraordinary. The Living A Meaning Life book series is a powerful story, and journey, of one such 'family' who dared to be extraordinary. By looking past their own obstacles in life, and choosing to always 'do the right things,' they became extraordinary within themselves, and this resulted in them doing extraordinary things that changed the lives of everyone around them, and their community. The main characters must navigate life struggles, both personal, and community oriented. They do so by 'doing the right things,' through exhibiting integrity, decency, generosity, and compassion. Life is never easy, people make mistakes, but there is nothing that can't be overcome when we have the courage to do what we know is correct and true within our soul.

The Hunter Equation is a practical spirituality book covering many topics, including life after death, reincarnation theory, cycle of life and death, human and animal souls, destiny vs. free will, synchronicities, Karma, soul mates, twin flames, angels, alien life, the future of humans, and many more topics. This is also the original book to unveil and fully explain the Hunter Equation life tool, and why it is far more relevant and accurate than The Law of Attraction.

love

Printed in Great Britain
by Amazon

85100861R00093